# What Journalists Are Owed

The study of news and news practice is rich in examinations of what journalists owe to society. However, this book looks at what journalists can expect from society: what roles ownership structures, colleagues, governments and audiences should play so journalists can do their jobs well – and safely.

*What Journalists Are Owed* draws on a variety of research perspectives – legal and ethical analysis, surveys, interviews and content analysis – in different national settings to look at how those relationships among stakeholders are developing in a time of rapid and often unsettling change to the political and economic environments that surround journalism. Journalism can be a risky business. This book opens some discussions on how those risks can be described and mitigated.

There's no shortage of writing about what journalists owe society – but if society wants journalism done well, what does it owe journalists in return? This volume opens a discussion on the cultural, legal-system and professional agreements that societies should provide so journalists can do their jobs in increasingly hostile political environments.

This book was originally published as a special issue of *Journalism Studies*.

**Fred Vultee** is an Associate Professor at the Department of Communication at Wayne State University, Detroit, USA.

**Lee Wilkins** is a Professor Emerita at the Department of Communication at Wayne State University, Detroit, USA, and Professor Emerita at the School of Journalism at the University of Missouri, Columbia, USA.

## Journalism Studies: Theory and Practice

*Series editor: Bob Franklin, Cardiff School of Journalism, Media and Cultural Studies, Cardiff University, UK*

The journal *Journalism Studies* was established at the turn of the new millennium by Bob Franklin. It was launched in the context of a burgeoning interest in the scholarly study of journalism and an expansive global community of journalism scholars and researchers. The ambition was to provide a forum for the critical discussion and study of journalism as a subject of intellectual inquiry but also an arena of professional practice. Previously, the study of journalism in the UK and much of Europe was a fairly marginal branch of the larger disciplines of media, communication and cultural studies; only a handful of Universities offered degree programmes in the subject. *Journalism Studies* has flourished and succeeded in providing the intended public space for discussion of research on key issues within the field, to the point where in 2007 a sister journal, *Journalism Practice*, was launched to enable an enhanced focus on practice-based issues, as well as foregrounding studies of journalism education, training and professional concerns. Both journals are among the leading ranked journals within the field and publish six issues annually, in electronic and print formats. More recently, 2013 witnessed the launch of a further companion journal *Digital Journalism* to provide a site for scholarly discussion, analysis and responses to the wide ranging implications of digital technologies for the practice and study of journalism. From the outset, the publication of themed issues has been a commitment for all journals. Their purpose is first, to focus on highly significant or neglected areas of the field; second, to facilitate discussion and analysis of important and topical policy issues; and third, to offer readers an especially high quality and closely focused set of essays, analyses and discussions.

The *Journalism Studies: Theory and Practice* book series draws on a wide range of these themed issues from all journals and thereby extends the critical and public forum provided by them. The Editor of the journals works closely with guest editors to ensure that the books achieve relevance for readers and the highest standards of research rigour and academic excellence. The series makes a significant contribution to the field of journalism studies by inviting distinguished scholars, academics and journalism practitioners to discuss and debate the central concerns within the field. It also reaches a wider readership of scholars, students and practitioners across the social sciences, humanities and communication arts, encouraging them to engage critically with, but also to interrogate, the specialist scholarly studies of journalism which this series provides.

Recent titles in the series:

**Writing the First World War after 1918**
*Edited by Adrian Bingham*

**The Future of Journalism: Risks, Threats and Opportunities**
*Edited by Stuart Allan, Cynthia Carter, Stephen Cushion, Lina Dencik, Iñaki Garcia-Blanco, Janet Harris, Richard Sambrook, Karin Wahl-Jorgensen and Andy Williams*

For more information about this series, please visit: https://www.routledge.com/Journalism-Studies/book-series/JOURNALISM

# What Journalists Are Owed

## How Structures, Systems and Audiences Enable News Work Today


*Edited by*

**Fred Vultee and Lee Wilkins**



Routledge
Taylor & Francis Group
LONDON AND NEW YORK

First published 2020
by Routledge
2 Park Square, Milton Park, Abingdon, Oxon, OX14 4RN

and by Routledge
52 Vanderbilt Avenue, New York, NY 10017

*Routledge is an imprint of the Taylor & Francis Group, an informa business*



*British Library Cataloguing-in-Publication Data*
A catalogue record for this book is available from the British Library

ISBN13: 978-0-367-43790-9

Typeset in Myriad Pro
by codeMantra

**Publisher's Note**
The publisher accepts responsibility for any inconsistencies that may have arisen during the conversion of this book from journal articles to book chapters, namely the inclusion of journal terminology.

# Contents

# Citation Information

The chapters in this book were originally published in *Journalism Studies*, volume 18, issue 1 (January 2017). When citing this material, please use the original page numbering for each article, as follows:

**Introduction**
*Duties, Rights and Election-Night Pizza: Toward an Agenda of "What Journalists Are Owed"*
Fred Vultee and Lee Wilkins
*Journalism Studies*, volume 18, issue 1 (January 2017) pp. 1–10

**Chapter 1**
*All in the Game: Communitarianism and* The Wire
Chad Painter
*Journalism Studies*, volume 18, issue 1 (January 2017) pp. 11–27

**Chapter 2**
*What Does Society Owe Political Cartoonists?*
Jenn Burleson Mackay
*Journalism Studies*, volume 18, issue 1 (January 2017) pp. 28–44

**Chapter 3**
*The Networks of Global Journalism: Global News Construction Through the Collaboration of Global News Startups with Freelancers*
Lea Hellmueller, Sadia Ehsan Cheema, and Xu Zhang
*Journalism Studies*, volume 18, issue 1 (January 2017) pp. 45–64

**Chapter 4**
*Pakistani Government-News Media Relationships: How Relevant Are Western Journalistic Values?*
Nadeem Akhtar and Cornelius B. Pratt
*Journalism Studies*, volume 18, issue 1 (January 2017) pp. 65–85

**Chapter 5**
*Rearticulating* New York Times V. Sullivan *As A Social Duty to Journalists*
Aimee Edmondson
*Journalism Studies*, volume 18, issue 1 (January 2017) pp. 86–101

**Chapter 6**

*Watching Over the Watchdogs: The Problems that Filipino Journalists Face*
Edson C. Tandoc Jr.
*Journalism Studies*, volume 18, issue 1 (January 2017) pp. 102–117

For any permission-related enquiries please visit:
http://www.tandfonline.com/page/help/permissions

# Contributors

**Nadeem Akhtar**, School of Business Administration, South China University of Technology, China, and Department of Journalism and Mass Communication, Kohat University of Science and Technology, Pakistan.

**Sadia Ehsan Cheema**, College of Media and Communication, Texas Tech University, Lubbock, USA.

**Aimee Edmondson**, E. W. Scripps School of Journalism, Ohio University, Athens, USA.

**Lea Hellmueller**, Jack J. Valenti School of Communication, University of Houston, USA.

**Jenn Burleson Mackay**, Department of Communication, Virginia Tech, USA.

**Chad Painter**, Department of Communication, University of Dayton, USA.

**Cornelius B. Pratt**, Department of Strategic Communication, School of Media and Communication, Temple University, Philadelphia, USA.

**Edson C. Tandoc Jr.**, Wee Kim Wee School of Communication and Information, Nanyang Technological University, Singapore.

**Xu Zhang**, Journalism and Electronic Media, University of Tennessee, Knoxville, USA.

**INTRODUCTION**

# DUTIES, RIGHTS AND ELECTION-NIGHT PIZZA

## Toward an agenda of "what journalists are owed"

**Fred Vultee** and **Lee Wilkins**

We're Fred Vultee and Lee Wilkins (in alphabetical order), your Guest Editors for this special issue. We're both former journalists, and we've been arguing about topics like this one for quite some time—well before we found ourselves working together at Wayne State University. This introduction took shape by email, phone calls and occasionally bursting into each other's offices waving a freshly printed copy of the latest dead-parrot routine from the genuinely unusual US political cycle of 2015–2016. Indeed, the great challenge of putting together a set of arguments on the topic of "what journalists are owed" has been separating the episodic hilarity and outrage that journalism is heir to from the systemic concerns that inspired our original interest, much as they also inspired the painstaking work of the authors whose attention was caught by fine details of that broad subject. We'll introduce those authors and their topics as they come up in the conversation, because we do view this as a conversation, and we'd be grateful—as analog journalists now charged with guiding journalism students into a digital age—if you in turn will pick up your end: engage with us, or with the authors whose work we're fortunate to present here, or with each other.

By random selection ($F[1,1]$, $p = 0.5$), Lee gets to go first.

**Wilkins:** Much scholarship on journalism and ethics, whether it is from the critical/cultural perspective or is based in philosophically informed theory, focuses on what journalists owe "us" as individuals or "us" as members of a social and political community. The thinking, particularly in the United States, has been that with the gift of the First Amendment, a privilege enjoyed by few other groups, comes obligation. The First Amendment is uniquely American; the foundational assertion that it represents—that democracies can function only with robust conversations among multiple stakeholders—owes a debt to documents that are as historical as the Magna Carta and as contemporary as the Universal Declaration of Human Rights. That foundation has international cachet. The sense of obligation that comes with it has permeated the profession itself, at least since the early 1900s, when Walter Williams penned the Journalists' Creed beginning with the affirmation: "journalism is a public service." This connection between journalism and democratic functioning is accepted by this issue's editors, and we believe many of its readers as well.

However, there are complexities. In the United States, this view of a single profession—journalism as a public service and journalism as a profit-making enterprise—has fueled some of the most intense, and some have said intractable, academic debates in the past half century. Academic study suggests that this American-centric view—that journalism can not only pay for itself, but also make a great deal of money in the process while serving the public good—has left North America and become acceptable in many places. Paying for journalism in novel ways has itself become a cottage industry. In many places and in many ways, what people and governments pay for, they want to control; there is no other obligation. This tension—between making money and public service—is at the core of many professional struggles today.

But outside of the efforts to monetize content, there have been human costs. Since 1992, more than 1000 journalists have died in the midst of pursuing a story. Some deaths have been horrifyingly public. Whether it is the multiple beheadings that have occurred, the "disappeared" journalists reporting on drug cartels, or those who have died at their own hands, no other civilian professionals—perhaps with the exception of the clergy—are asked to give their lives to perform a societally acknowledged role. We make jokes about "killing all the lawyers," but journalists are distinctively singled out for the sort of physical and verbal violence that this death toll represents. The privilege of the First Amendment and the foundational assumptions on which it is based make journalists special. It is our contention that it should not make them dead.

So we begin the special issue of *Journalism Studies* with a point/counterpoint discussion between the editors about what it is that journalists themselves are owed. And, to begin, I will make the seemingly obvious statement: our employers owe journalists both the time to think and the time to mature. I'll amplify after Fred takes the floor.

**Vultee:** I certainly won't disagree with the obligation of time to think. I'll even go one better than the gift of room to grow and to make mistakes—I'd like all my successors in the newsroom to be able to travel back in time and make their worst mistakes without an internet to spread them around the world. I won't say I made all my journalistic blunders in a vacuum, but I certainly made the bulk of them in a smaller echo chamber.

It's cherry-picking to lean on the aspects of the interactive age that I like with one hand and shove the internet away with the other: yes, I want to have my cake and my diet too. But that tension between technology and news work—when it helps us and when it gets in the way—is at the core of a lot of bigger tensions. The stories that need to be told about police–civilian interactions couldn't be told if interactive technology wasn't everywhere, but we need room to separate those stories from every celebrity feud that "went viral," without regard to audience metrics—as well as room to hold citizen journalism up to the same critical assessment as our own output.

Journalists are entitled to a different relationship with their everyday audience—I say this having tended to calls from the angry regulars on many an evening and weekend—than with the first-time readers who drop in with a few dozen of their favorite racist comments because a story has been linked on some prominent bottom-feeding linkblog. That means journalists are owed an opportunity to go against the audience-at-all-costs gospel of interactivity, and here I want to push the period of economic tension a little farther back than you do. The Hutchins Commission's "free and responsible press" report came out in 1947, but the idea of the Commission arose in 1942 and reflects deep concerns lingering from what had been (for Americans) the prewar period and the powerful isolationist press that seemed to rule public opinion. The report puts a lot of responsibility on the press to provide accurate information in a meaningful context, because it also places a lot of weight on the audience to do its democratic work competently. (Chad Painter's "All in the Game" puts that mutual obligation in a context of communitarianism: how stakeholders can address the institutional breakdowns that afflict journalism and other social structures.) When we say journalists are owed the time to think about their work, we imply that we're ready to accept some of their conclusions. If that means disabling comments on all news stories unto the end of time, fine. I don't think that's substantively different from the right to not be surrounded by advertisements for miracle cures, Europorn and survival food.

We're not the only craft that's entitled to decent surroundings. I finally saw Paul Simon perform in concert this summer, nearly five decades after buying my first Paul Simon record. About three songs in, he told the people in the expensive seats to stop batting things around—"kill the beach ball," or words to that effect. I'm aware of the commercial mandate to address the audience's interests (and meeting those interests has helped make many house payments)—but I think we serve the core audience's needs better when we are free to tell the fringe audience to kill the beach ball.

Are we owed a job? That's the first topic that came up among old newspaper colleagues when I floated the call on social media for this issue. Even if I still wanted my three slices of lukewarm pizza between editions on election night, those jobs are largely gone. The assembly line simply doesn't work that way anymore. (Jenn Burleson Mackay's "What Does Society Owe Political Cartoonists?" addresses those changes in employment patterns among others in the web of challenges created by modern-day journalism.) I do think we're owed a management structure that's genuinely independent—bound neither by official regulation nor by journalistic tradition—in looking for ways to fund journalism in a livable way. If some repentant oil baron wants to endow a position in the statehouse bureau, or if broadband providers want to spread a 1 percent content-creation surcharge among news outlets in the communities they serve, I want to hear about it. We are owed a chance to be judged by the character of our content, not the color of our money.

But because you started with the First Amendment, let me raise something that I think our international colleagues are owed: an explanation of why we in the United States treat the First Amendment the way we do—whether universally unfettered speech is the boundless virtue we make it out to be, or whether it's one of those bits of American exceptionalism, like the death penalty and near-unlimited handgun ownership, that seem to afflict the afflicted even as the comfortable simply get more comfortable. I can look out my office window and see a country—Canada—that legally restricts hate speech, and I'd have a hard time demonstrating that their democracy suffers unduly for it. I wonder if journalists working outside the First Amendment's umbrella are owed some assurance that those of us under it remember Justice Robert Jackson's caution in Terminiello v. Chicago (a postwar case that involved a violent collision of anti-Semitic conspiracy theories, planned counterdemonstrations and police authority to keep order): "No liberty is made more secure by holding that its abuses are inseparable from its enjoyment."

**Wilkins:** I want to return to something Fred said and amplify it: "We are owed a chance to be judged by the character of our content, and not the color of our money." I'll add, we owe this to each other as much as the larger political and social community owes it to us. In true journalistic fashion, let me illustrate with an anecdote.

Journalist Curt Guyette, who has worked for multiple news organizations during his 20-year career, is widely credited with breaking the "Flint water story." This was an investigative project that reported the city of Flint, Michigan, for financial reasons, had switched the city water supply from the city of Detroit (which gets its water from a lake) to the Flint

River. When the city switched its water source, it failed to add a set of chemicals to the water that would have forestalled the corrosion of the lead pipes in the city's water infrastructure. The result: many of the city's residents, including about 7000 children, were exposed to lead in their drinking water supply. Since lead is a heavy metal and highly toxic in even small amounts, the result was a widespread and serious public health problem in a community that is poor and populated largely by people of color. Guyette's reporting helped to break this story, which resulted in the firing or resignation of government officials, Congressional hearings, criminal indictments, and ongoing discussions in the state of Michigan about the political arrangements that are—depending on politics—either a great deal or somewhat responsible for poisoning Flint residents. The Flint story is a classic example of what investigative reporters describe as a "system story"; it is local journalism that made a nationwide impact. Other cities, from New York to Portland, Oregon, have begun to test their water as a result.

So, and as one would expect to be the case, Guyette's work was nominated for a Pulitzer Prize. Here is where what we owe each other became an issue: the Pulitzer Committee declined to consider the nomination. Not because the journalism was poor or unheralded, but because Guyette's employer was the American Civil Liberties Union and hence his work was viewed as "advocacy journalism." This from an organization that gives awards for editorial writing and public service journalism. In the case of the Pulitzer Committee, apparently whoever signs the paycheck matters more than the content. (For those journalists who are reading this, Guyette told all of this to me recently; for the scholars among us, it would be cited as Curt Guyette, personal communication, April 8, 2016, Detroit, Michigan.)

My point here is one of professional solidarity—in the face of economic landslides and government assaults, not to mention the dangers imposed by reporting on war, drugs and corruption, which is both vast and banal. Who signs your paycheck—whether it's Fox or Greenpeace—should matter less than the quality of work that you do, at least in the view of one media ethicist. Guyette's loyalties were clearly to the public, to public service and to encouraging a debate about the impact of money in politics: not in the sense of who gets elected, but what happens after politicians holding public office find themselves making difficult decisions where dollars are balanced against quality of life. This is what journalism does. We owe it to each other to recognize it as such. (In "The Networks of Global Journalism," Lea Hellmueller, Sadia Ehsan Cheema, and Xu Zhang examine how one chronically underserved area, international news, is being affected by new economic models.)

The lack of attention to Guyette's work represents one form of a breakdown of that solidarity. But on this shrinking planet, I also would like to encourage our news organizations and us as individuals to acknowledge those who have helped us more systematically and more conscientiously than we currently do. Journalists would not be able to cover international stories were it not for those who translate and "fix"—travel arrangements, interviews, etc. Yet, those who help are seldom acknowledged as contributors to the final work on even a semi-equal footing. Sometimes, there is a good reason for that—on some stories, those who help journalists (and their families) are likely to be targeted and killed. But in other cases, we take credit where it is not due. In the world of the Web, making stories (even the print versions of broadcast reports) longer by these few words of acknowledgement would seem not just appropriate but required.

**Vultee:** What, you're asking a copy editor to give credit to the invisible people who make the product appear on schedule? I would agree even if I didn't see a personal stake. Much of our dialogue here focuses on individual initiative or disregard of danger, and we need to continue supporting that—and the awards that honor it, whatever we think of any individual Pulitzer decision. But journalism is still a team sport.

If I could rephrase what you're saying a bit: we may not be owed jobs individually, but we are owed a profession: a structure that lets journalists produce the sort of news that allows the audience to do its democratic job. Along with the time to think about what they're doing, that means journalists are owed the time and space to be routine. By "routine," I don't mean "boring"—I mean doing lots of small things right, no matter how few people are watching. Like baseball, journalism is "a game of the long season, of relentless and gradual averaging-out" (Updike 1960).

I'm glad you brought up the Flint case, because the smallest newspaper to win a Pulitzer for public service—the *Washington* (NC) *Daily News*—did so largely because somebody read the back of a water bill. There was a note about water test results that seemed worth checking out, and one thing led to another, and eventually what the *New York Times* called "an eight-year environmental cover-up" of carcinogens in a small town's water supply came unraveled. You can read a lot of fine print, and stay all the way to the end of a lot of tedious procedural meetings, and never run across a scandal—and that's fine. The night watch makes a lot of rounds that end with "all is well." But competent watchdoggery requires an economic structure in which your boss acknowledges that "reading the fine print" is a perfectly good answer to "what have you been doing all day?"

Solidarity has to work in a number of directions: between front of the camera and back of the camera, between the editor who has to count daily word output and the writer who might not produce any words for another week, and from side to side in the briefing room. That's going to raise some conflicts about what journalists are owed—or perhaps more precisely, when and under what circumstances we have a claim on some goods.

I wouldn't want to claim that we're owed an audience, and I think this is as true for would-be scholars as for would-be journalists. Freedom of expression is a right; an audience is earned. But to get back to the amphitheater for a moment, I do think the audience is obliged to judge us by what's on the playbill. If you want to boo Paul Simon for the rearrangement of "Homeward Bound," that's your right (you're wrong, of course, but the First Amendment treats all opinions equally). But you can't boo Paul Simon for not being Ozzy Osbourne. That isn't the ticket you bought. Bear in mind, we're not just entertaining an audience—we're supposedly arming it against people who would work against its interests.

Are we owed an interview? I'm even less sure about that. We're owed the documents (at least, in most cases, the public ones), but journalism is a social transaction before it is a legal one. The man in the street, and the woman leaving the polling place, do us a favor when they provide the quotation that supports our interpretation of the survey data. By extension, I'm not sure I'm ready to stand in solidarity with that character from the opposition outlet demanding that the candidate explain whether he's stopped selling drugs to schoolchildren.

**Wilkins:** [Interrupts] Fred, in a democracy, elected public officials do owe us an interview. I'll go one further and say that business officials—from the CEO of Intel to the local entrepreneur—also owe us an interview. The average citizen whom we seek out—perhaps not so much. But, the person who posts racist and/or sexist or homophobic or revolutionary comments on a website—they need to be accountable to the rest of us as well. Public speech is more than a purely commercial transaction. To quote mass communication scholar James Carey, "Journalism is a political act." That extends to those who are a part —or refuse to be a part—of it, including audience members who share their thinking with others using our stories as a springboard to do so. Okay, now back to Fred.

**Vultee:** I appreciate the principle, but isn't there a risk in conflating bulk with substance? If every outlet insists on getting an in-person explanation of why the candidate's apparent racism is really The Media's fault, how is the sixth identical explanation better than the first—except in giving the candidate more control over the day's discourse? At some point, when the guy says "If that makes me a bigot, you can call me a bigot," we should think about honoring his request.

I know we're having a hard time keeping this conversation on the big picture and away from current events, but when one candidate tells another that he's tired of hearing about her damn emails, I don't feel that reflexive journalistic urge to disagree with him. And because the 2016 campaign recalls the build-a-higher-wall nationalism of the original America First era, I'm reminded of the time when Franklin D. Roosevelt (FDR) brought an Iron Cross to a news conference to give to a particularly anti-FDR reporter (who was himself in the middle of a lawsuit against another paper that had called him a "naziphile"). The isolationist camp reported on the horrified reaction among the press, but you have to wonder if there might have been a little cheering in the press box, too.

**Wilkins:** Okay, so I'm not going to resist the current American "silly season," which is what American political reporters call our every-four-year spasm and constitutionally required general election. In the United States, when Donald Trump rescinds the press credentials of a legitimate news organization such as the *Washington Post*, we owe each other support. This support should be evident in at least two ways. First, we should report it. That's the easy part. Second, we should stand in solidarity with that other news organization—we should raise the issue at every opportunity and we should be willing to "walk out" or find an alternative such as "pool coverage" to serve notice that, in a democracy, the citizenry is owed a response and that response comes through journalists doing journalism. Trump is also free to tweet on his own—that, too, is a First Amendment guarantee, and another way of responding to citizens. He's even free to buy a newspaper or television station (s) and promulgate his views in that way. But, what the profession should contest is Trump's willingness to muzzle others all the while insisting on his First Amendment rights. We can only do that by working cooperatively; competition, here, is misplaced and professionally disadvantages all—even Fox News, although that organization may not realize it. Journalists professionally have not done a good job articulating the connections and rewards of professional community, something that doctors, lawyers and the clergy have mastered to a much greater degree. We need to learn from them. And, internationally, we need to involve our colleagues who work in democracies—or battle for democratic government—in finding multiple ways to explain that this link between journalism and democratic functioning is crucial and has implications beyond the borders of a nation-state. (Nadeem Akhtar and Cornelius B. Pratt explore those tensions between journalists and the people and institutions they cover in "Pakistani Government–News Media Relationships.")

**Vultee:** Let me clarify—the public is owed public presentations by public people (though I'm not at all sure they're owed an interview with the victim's partner at the crime scene). And the legal–political–social structure owes journalists the room to talk *about* public people, whether those people talk *to* us or not. (Aimee Edmondson's "Rearticulating *New York Times* v. Sullivan as a Social Duty to Journalists" suggests how recently won that obligation is—and, given some political figures, how tenuous it could be.) I'm wondering, though, if every news organization is owed every interview it asks for—or even if the end result of that would be a good idea. The *Washington Post* has every right to be in the room or on the plane, but at some point the best response to a grade-school temper tantrum might be the front-page editorial cartoon. I wish there was more daylight between the right to an interview and the right to demand the long-form birth certificate, because I'm not sure I can claim the first without granting the second.

I really don't think the framers of the Constitution would go along with guaranteeing Twitter access. There's a kind of a cottage industry in the United States these days built around complaining that free speech is threatened when some social media platform or another tweaks an algorithm to push the Murdoch papers' favorite scandal down the agenda, and we don't have to pay those complaints much heed, either. If you want to promote a viewpoint (regardless of whether it's available 24 hours a day, with occasional breaks for traffic and weather, on over-the-air radio), you can buy a soapbox. You don't have a right to break into someone else's garage and steal theirs.

**Wilkins:** There's also a second element of solidarity I want to explore. That example comes directly from thinking about ethics: we need to be willing to cry "foul" when a group or organization claims to be a journalist or claims to be doing journalism that is in clear violation of the profession's ethical standards—even as those standards are being debated. The fact that professionally we cannot agree on what constitutes ethical behavior in every instance should not blind us to the fact that there is vast agreement on some things that "are not good journalism." For example, it is not ethical journalism to edit video in such a way as to make people out to say what they do not mean and have explicitly contradicted. It is not good journalism to deliberately add facts or distort them for the purposes of deceiving the public. Being willing to label some things "not ethical journalism" should be a professional response to that which diminishes the work that journalists do and do well. And, it gives us a way to discuss the gray areas—advocacy such as that exemplified by Guyette or the withholding of some sorts of information (for various reasons and in contrast to fabricating information or making a mistake). Those discussions are important; but they are no more important than being willing to say, professionally and publicly, this act is beyond the pale. From my point of view, pointing out our professional shortcomings has been one of the truly enlightening elements of political satire—whether it's Jonathan Swift or Jon Stewart. Even the academy has contributed here: examining patterns of coverage, from AIDS not making the front page of the *New York Times* until a decade into the epidemic to noting that the *Guardian* conducts its own ethics audit once a year … it all helps us improve the public service component of what we do.

**Vultee:** There's more to it than just satire—the United States really doesn't have a tradition of sustained, well-informed press commentary. I think we're owed a strong corps of critics as surely as music and theater are: not just people who yell and scream about "media bias," but people who can measure biases in their context through knowing how the craft of journalism works. (A. J. Liebling was a matchless press critic because he was, in his words, an "incurable, recidivist reporter.")

Broad agreement on ethical ground rules is better than no agreement, and journalists should be as intolerant of deception from their own ranks as they are of deception from the podium. But I think we need a little more guidance to get through the one-man's-terrorist problem, and that's why autonomy is about not being bound by what the competition, or the news agencies or networks, are doing as much as it is about independence from commercial pressure. Think of the dilemma faced by the newspaper reporters in Tim Crouse's wonderful account of the 1972 presidential campaign (Crouse 1973): the editors at home want something fresh, not the same story everyone else has, but when the fresh story arrives, they demand to know why it isn't the same story the agencies provided.

Independent means independent: not what Joseph Pulitzer or Walter Williams or the station across town would do, but what the evidence and your decision-making structure tell you to do. There's a strong professional bias against ignoring someone else's scandal. Once somebody turns the owner's pet anecdote into a "-gate," it's hard not to join in, but we need the professional space and support to, every now and then, say no. That's not a story, and I'm not spending time, brain cells or server space on it today.

It's important that you brought up the physical dangers, because one reason I have room to grouse at length about professional autonomy is that I don't have to worry about the government jailing me, or asking its friends to drag me out of my car for a beating, or mysteriously doubling the price of newsprint for me and no one else. (Edson C. Tandoc's "Watching Over the Watchdogs" looks at how Filipino journalists assess such threats to their profession as violence, information access and pay structures.) Without trying to minimize the real physical risks that many journalists face, I'd also say more broadly that we're owed a noncombatant status in the culture wars as well as the political wars—the right to not draw grand moral conclusions about what we bring to public attention.

As with much of our discussion here, I'm drawing on what we see as we're writing. We can explain what the Brexit vote means, but I'd like to be excused from standing with the commentator who cheers on the triumph of 1930s-style nationalism as the European Union stumbles toward joining the Soviet Union on the ash heap of history. Journalists are entitled to go into great detail about the process and its details, but they're also entitled to be Morgenthau-style realists: to explain what happened without presuming that their publisher's worldview aligns with the moral laws of the universe.

**Wilkins:** Well, since I have had the publisher stand over my shoulder as I was editing a story about one of the paper's biggest advertisers, to be frank, I worry a lot less about that sort of encounter than I do the power of government and of large corporate entities to forestall or obfuscate public discussion through the news media. And, I also worry—a lot—about the audience's ability to ignore such blatant manipulation. Fred, you said an audience must be earned. So, too, must democracy. Journalists and journalism can't earn that form of government alone. Democracy, too, is a team sport.

**Vultee:** We've been saying "we" a lot, so let me shift gears for a moment and ask what you think we in the academy owe to journalists. That's at least a two-part question: what we do in the classroom and what we do in the lab. I have to tell you, I'm disappointed to look at survey results and see that academic research falls pretty low on the list of things journalists look to for information about their profession. Journalists don't seem to think they are owed more scholarship—should we try to change that perception, or should we just leave well enough alone?

**Wilkins:** So, back to the "what are journalists owed" question, I think the academy owes them two things. The first, and for those journalists who come to us for training, we owe our best efforts to link theory to professional practice in ways large and small. We need to let students know that the leads they write are all about "framing." We need to tell videographers that we don't know much about how audiences interpret images … but we are working on it. We need to ask the big questions: why, when confronted with facts about things such as climate change, are some audience members routinely and predictably willing to discount "the facts" for an alternate interpretation that makes no logical or scientific sense but obviously makes sense to that person.

Second, as a group that has been granted the gift of time to think, the academy owes journalists and journalism the gift of "the moral imagination": not in the sense that professors have it and others don't, but in the sense that professors have more time to systematically explore the implications. What's going to replace objectivity as a professional standard? Are there innovative experiments in paying for journalism that can begin "on the quad," then find their way into the world? Are there universal ethical norms that persist despite culture or political system? Can news be "done" as virtual reality—and how does that technology change our news routines as well as how the audience interprets that "story"? And, is storytelling really the best description for Curt Guyette's efforts, or should we invent a new verb that owes less to Hollywood and more to Edward R. Murrow and Edward Snowden?

**Vultee:** Maybe this is one good thing to emerge from the technological and economic wreckage of the past decade. We're confronted with the need to rethink a lot of rules and assumptions, and out of that, we're all—working journalists, students and faculty members—owed a chance to see that any such rethinking makes sense. I'm thinking specifically about a class some years ago that was reviewing the Associated Press's (AP's) (then new) social media guidelines. One guideline had to do with quoting Twitter: something to the effect of, OK, but make sure you verify by phone. One of the students asked: what about a verified Twitter account—could I quote directly from that? Understand, it's an editing course, and our default is often "never answer style questions that begin with 'why.'" Once I got over that, it was a good question—and more to the point, it was a good professional question. This student wasn't trying to dodge the rules. He was looking for a way to practice the discipline of verification in the technical-social context of the career he was about to have, rather than the one I used to have. We need to distinguish technological get-off-my-lawnism from the principles that smart, autonomous journalists will use to make sense of Twitter as well as the Next Big Thing after Twitter. The point is "verify," not "verify on a rotary-dial telephone."

That's true of micro-rules too. If journalists are going to be expected to follow a style manual, it needs to make sense for real-life use. I like the *Guardian*'s frankness in having a style guide that admittedly reflects its cultural values, and I think journalists deserve that kind of openness, rather than a claim that some social choice in language or another is the "precise" way to speak about social groups or conditions. And—speaking for my fellow copy editors here—we probably owe both reporters and students an admission. Some of the stuff we've yelled about over the years basically amounts to a set of secret handshakes that signify membership in the Ancient and Mystic Order of People with Too Much Time on Their Hands. Yes, I'm in the camp that could care less (Walsh 2013) about the AP allowing "over" to mean "more than"; think of all the brain cells that can now go to doing journalism.

**Wilkins:** Okay, enough of us. There are other, very smart and articulate people, who have responses to this question as well. To foreshadow that portion of the discussion, we turn to the remainder of this special issue.

**Vultee:** And let me conclude by thanking the authors for the diversity of ideas and perspectives they bring to the question of what journalists are owed. There are projects based on content categories and on occupational categories; ethics-based explorations springing from the portrayal of journalism in fiction and from the changing role of the commentator; surveys that let journalists speak for themselves and interviews that let news innovators speak for themselves; and a legal-historical reminder that the past isn't as different a country as we might like to think. We're grateful to Editor Bob Franklin for letting us borrow his journal, and we encourage you all to turn to the menu and join the discussion.

## DISCLOSURE STATEMENT

No potential conflict of interest was reported by the authors.

## REFERENCES

Crouse, Timothy. 1973. *The Boys on the Bus*. New York: Ballantine.

Updike, John. 1960. Hub Fans Bid Kid Adieu. *The New Yorker*, October 22. Accessed July 22, 2016. http://www.newyorker.com/magazine/1960/10/22/hub-fans-bid-kid-adieu.

Walsh, Bill. 2013. *Yes, I Could Care Less: How to be a Language Snob without Being a Jerk*. New York: St, Martin's.

# ALL IN THE GAME
## Communitarianism and *The Wire*

**Chad Painter**

*Communitarian ethicists argue that social identity is formed by community relationships, emphasizing the connection between an individual and his or her community. News organizations are part of that community. Indeed, journalism only functions properly in terms of the public and public life, and as part of a larger community. This textual analysis study focused on the breakdown of the fictional Baltimore community depicted in the television series* The Wire. *Five institutions—the police force and justice system, the labor force, local and state politicians and government, the educational system, and the daily newspaper—have failed, and, in turn, the city is failing. Through the lens of communitarian ethics, the researcher argues that community stakeholders must recognize the need for a strong community from which the press can operate to report, explain, correct, and connect.*

### Introduction

The public often decries the lack of media coverage surrounding certain events. The organization Project Censored, for example, is dedicated to uncovering stories unreported —or under-reported—by the mainstream media. However, there are several stories that *are* covered by the media that simply are not consumed by the public: for example, the water crisis in Flint, Michigan. Journalists from the *Flint Journal* wrote more than 500 stories about the city's water crisis during a two-year period starting in January 2014 (Hiner 2016). As John Hiner, vice president of content at MLive Media Group and the former executive editor at the *Flint Journal*, wrote in a letter to Poynter, "From politics to public health implications to the impact on residents of this hurting city, there has been no development that has gone unreported or unexplained" (Hiner 2016, 1). The missing component of the story, according to Hiner, was people inside and outside of Michigan caring. He wrote that the story received "less total readership over 12 months than the Michigan–Michigan State football game" and that routine weather stories are more widely read than the Flint water crisis, even after a doctor raised the alarm in September 2015 about rising lead levels in children's blood (1).

A socially responsible press only makes sense in terms of the public and public life (Christians et al. 2009).

The media influence and are influenced by the larger social, cultural, legal, political, and economic systems in which they operate (Christians, Ferré, and Fackler 1993; Hallin and Mancini 2004). The central argument in this article is that journalism only functions properly as part of a larger community. Thus, citizens, elites, experts, governments, and other constituent groups owe journalists a community from which to monitor, facilitate, and collaborate. Citizens who participate actively with public life contribute to a "great community" (Dewey 1954). However, citizen voices are marginalized during public policy debates, and the business of media is placed outside the boundaries of democratic politics (McChesney 1999). Public discourse increasingly takes the form of entertainment (Postman 1985). Politics, religion, news, athletics, education, and commerce have been transformed into forms of show business, largely without much popular notice, let alone protest (Postman 1985).

The researcher will explore the breakdown of community through the fictional television series *The Wire*. On June 2, 2002, HBO aired the premier episode of *The Wire*, a sprawling and complex television drama that lasted for five seasons and 60 episodes. The Baltimore depicted in *The Wire* is a failing city. It is failing because five components important to the makeup of any city—the police force and justice system, the labor force depicted through unionized dockworkers, politicians at the local and state levels, the school system, and the city newspaper—are failing. Series creator David Simon has said that while Greek tragedies focus on the Gods, *The Wire* is about how people give God-like reverence to institutions (O'Rourke 2006). When these institutions fail, the community fails; and when community fails, the media cannot adequately perform their role in that society.

## Literature Review

### *Communitarianism and Public Discourse*

Communitarian ethicists emphasize the connection between an individual and his or her community, arguing that a person's social identity largely is formed by community relationships (Bell 1993; Delaney 1994; Tam 1998). Such ethicists propose that the community ought to secure a balance between individual autonomy and the common good. Philosophically, modern communitarianism is rooted in the work of John Dewey, who wrote:

> Individuals are interdependent. No one is born except in dependence on others ... The human being is an individual because of and in relations with others. Otherwise, he is an individual only as a stick of wood is, namely, as spatially and numerically separate. (Dewey 1985, 227)

Communitarians, then, seek a balance between individual rights and social responsibilities, believing that the self is neither autonomous nor exists in isolation (Etzioni 1993). Instead, the self is shaped by values and culture of interdependent communities (Etzioni 1993).

Culbertson and Chen (1997) propose six core tenets of communitarianism: (1) the rightness or wrongness of a behavior depends in large part on its positive contribution to commitment to and quality of relationships (37–38); (2) community requires a sense of interconnectedness and social cohesion (38); (3) identification of, and humble but firm commitment to, core values and beliefs are essential to a sense of community (38–39); (4) people who claim rights must be willing to balance them with responsibilities (39); (5) community requires that all citizens have a feeling of empowerment, of involvement in making and implementing decisions that bear on their lives (39–40); finally, (6) community requires a broadening of one's social world, one's array of significant others, so as to reduce fragmentation and enhance breadth of perspective (40).

These communities sometimes can be physical, such as a religious congregation or parent–teacher association. Community demands a place where people can see and know each other, where children can learn and play, and where adults work and engage in leisure activities together (Sandel 1996). Etzioni (1993) argued that two basic characteristics form a community. The first is a web of crisscrossing and reinforcing relationships among a group of individuals. The second is shared culture, values, norms, history, and identity. However, communities often are imagined, socially constructed by people thinking about themselves as belonging to some larger group (Anderson 2006). A nation, for example, is an imagined community: "imagined" because it is impossible to know even a large minority of fellow-members, and a "community" because it is conceived in terms of deep comradeship (Anderson 2006). Dewey (1954) argued that publics are spontaneous groups of citizens who share the indirect effects of a particular action. Anyone affected by the indirect consequences of a specific action, therefore, will have a common interest in solving a common problem. As part of a public, people have certain inescapable claims on each other that cannot be renounced except at the cost of their humanity (Christians, Ferré, and Fackler 1993).

One such inescapable claim, according to Dewey (1954), is to engage in politics and political discourse, the work and duty of each individual in the course of his or her daily routine. Sandel (1996) argued that liberty, in the republican tradition, depends on self-government, which in turn depends on members of a political community identifying with the role of citizen and undertaking the obligations of citizenship. Liberty requires knowledge of public affairs, a sense of belonging, a concern for the whole, and a moral bond with the community (Sandel 1996). Communication is the key to a great community, and citizens who deliberate with fellow citizens about the common good help shape the destiny of the political community and contribute to that community (Dewey 1954; Sandel 1996). Such communication occurs in a public sphere, a space outside of state control where individuals exchange views and knowledge (Habermas 1991). The critical nature of a public sphere might expose citizens to conflicting views, which political scholars have deemed a necessary, albeit often missing, element of the kind of political dialogue needed to maintain democracy (Mutz and Martin 2001). There is a need to engage citizens in public deliberation, or discussions on complex policy issues, in a contemporary version of the public sphere (Guttman 2007).

Robert Putnam (2000) stressed the importance of bridging social capital, where bonds of connectedness are bridged across diverse social groups. However, he wrote that Americans increasingly are abandoning community, trading common identity and shared public life for individual pursuits (Putnam 2000). Participation in politics, civic affairs, religious worship, workplace connections, and philanthropy and volunteering started a downward trajectory in the 1970s, and this trajectory accelerated during the 1980s to 2000s (Putnam 2000). Consequently, social, political, and economic systems are failing.

### *Communitarianism and the Media*

Social responsibility theory is based on a communitarian model that seeks justice, covenant, and empowerment (Christians, Ferré, and Fackler 1993). The fourth component of communitarianism is an organizational culture that is based on mutuality (Christians, Ferré, and Fackler 1993). The ultimate goal of reporting becomes social transformation

(Christians, Ferré, and Fackler 1993) that could occur at the local, state, regional, national, or international level. Consequently, the media should elevate their standards by emphasizing alternatives, choices, consequences, and conditions to foster conversation, improve knowledge, and provide citizens with the material and guidance necessary for self-governance (Dewey 1954; Nerone 1995; Smith 1988). A media system based on social responsibility is premised on the idea that freedom of expression is a positive freedom (Berlin 2002; Nerone 1995). Expression is not an inalienable right, but an earned moral right (Nerone 1995). That moral right, and the nature of the press' freedom, is serving the public (Nerone 1995; The Commission on Freedom of the Press 1947). Proponents of a socially responsible press argue that the press only makes sense in terms of the public and public life, that the fundamental problem in journalism is the reconstitution of the public (Christians, Ferré, and Fackler 1993; Christians et al. 2009; Dewey 1954).

The media can create a space for civic engagement, the coming together of individuals and groups to discuss and address areas of mutual concern (Coleman et al. 2008). Increased civic engagement, in turn, can lead to higher levels of political and civic participation (Coleman et al. 2008). The press supports the maintenance of public space and public life by creating spaces where the public can address one another and by enhancing discourse in those public spaces (Carey 1997). One major purpose of the press is to promote and improve public life, not just report on it (Glasser and Craft 1997). Therefore, journalists must re-examine the traditional ideal of maintaining distance between themselves and the communities they serve by expanding the realm of individual debate to include themselves (Glasser and Craft 1997; Hodges 1997).

There certainly is a normative reason for the media to engage in civic and public life. However, there also is an economic reason. Newspapers are no longer central to public life and must be transformed before they become superfluous (Anderson, Dardenne, and Killenberg 1997). People or groups, such as the media, agree to provide needed services; the community, in turn, agrees to compensate them for the services and recognize their right to perform them (Gardner, Csikszentmihalyi, and Damon 2002). Such a mutually beneficial relationship creates an authentic alignment. A professional realm is authentically aligned when the values of the culture are in line with those of the domain (knowledge, skills, practices, rules, and values), when the expectations of stakeholders (consumers, citizens, corporate shareholders, and executives) match those of the field (the roles that individuals practice when working with symbols of the domain and institutions), and when the domain and the field are themselves in sync (Gardner, Csikszentmihalyi, and Damon 2002).

Social responsibility theory represents the triumph of community against the individual through a radical reconstruction of the relationship between communities and individuals (Nerone 1995). Individuals working together for the common good perpetuate communities; individuals do not create communities but instead are born into them (Hodges 1997). Ferré (1988, 201) argued that "to successfully counter individual autonomy, a normative ethics of news reporting must understand that both community and personhood are central to the nature of human being and democratic social life." Therefore, any normative ethics of news reporting must insist that both community and personhood are central to the nature of being human, that our account of what constitutes human existence will necessarily influence beliefs about the proper conduct of democratic government, and that the media stand at the center of those webs of meaning by which people understand and transform culture (Christians, Ferré, and Fackler 1993).

## *The Wire*

*The Wire* is a show about Baltimore, but the city stands for a microcosm of the struggles of contemporary America (Fisher 2013; Gurland-Baker 2013). In the end, the show focuses on the diminishing value of life in a post-industrial, consumer-capitalist society (Crosby 2013). The show conforms to the structure of television melodrama seen in the rest of popular television since the 1980s (Williams 2014). It does, however, move away from family and personal sagas, moving toward institutional connections; it therefore becomes a more complex and closure-deferring series that compares and contrasts many institutional worlds (Williams 2014). The narrative is spread nearly evenly across multiple characters, each of whom matters almost equally (Williams 2014). There is no single protagonist because the series is focused on institutions, not individuals (Williams 2014).

At its core, *The Wire* is a crime drama; however, the real criminal is the entire social system, not an individual (Zizek 2013). It is a cop show that uses genre expectations as a way to probe larger, institutional injustices (Williams 2014). As show creator David Simon writes:

> *The Wire* was not about Jimmy McNulty. Or Avon Barksdale. Or Marlo Stanfield, or Tommy Carcetti or Gus Haynes. It was not about crime. Or punishment. Or the drug war. Or politics. Or race. Or education, labor relations or journalism. It was about the city ... By showing a new aspect of a simulated American city in all its complexity, we might, by the end of the show's run, have a chance to speak to something more universal than Avon Barksdale or Jimmy McNulty or drugs or crime. (Simon 2009, 3, 28)

Each of the five seasons focuses on a different institutional aspect of the failing, though fictional, Baltimore. In Season 1, viewers see the failure of the war on drugs through the West Baltimore drug market that police cannot curtail (Alvarez 2009; Simon 2009; Williams 2014; Zizek 2013). Season 2 centers on the betrayal and disappearance of the blue-collar working class as seen through a failing, corrupt dockworkers union (Alvarez 2009; Simon 2009; Williams 2014; Zizek 2013). A cynical government and political culture raises then crushes hopes for reform in Season 3, where viewers see increasingly desperate police and political strategies to resolve the city's drug problem (Alvarez 2009; Simon 2009; Williams 2014; Zizek 2013). The state of public education is shown through the waste and failure of an urban school system to sufficiently educate a largely black underclass in Season 4 (Alvarez 2009; Simon 2009; Williams 2014; Zizek 2013). Finally, viewers see the slow, ugly death of the American newspaper that fails to report, explain, correct, or connect the institutional problems outlined in the previous four seasons (Alvarez 2009; Ferrucci and Painter 2014; Herbert 2012; Simon 2009; Williams 2014; Zizek 2013). Previous scholars have labeled the fifth season as one of the most truthful depictions of a newsroom in popular culture (Hanson 2008; Sabin 2011). Working journalists, however, have attacked Simon as vindictive and obsessed, arguing that the depiction of individual journalists, especially Scott Templeton, was at best distorted for entertainment purposes and at worst wholly inaccurate (Steiner 2013). These critiques marginalize Simon's attacks on corporatized newsrooms and the resultant loss of journalistic identity and credibility (Steiner 2013).

Institutions on *The Wire* are obsessed with quantifying victory (Fagan 2013), from the police department manipulating crime statistics and the educational system doing likewise with statewide testing scores, to the daily newspaper eschewing good reporting in favor of chasing a Pulitzer. These institutions, ultimately, harm both the individuals who comprise them and the individuals and communities they are meant to serve (Crosby 2013). Institutional forces that are nearly impossible to resist shape each character (Fagan 2013), and each season highlights individuals who are unequal to the problem or task they face (Schaub 2010). The series culminates with a montage that drives the point that nothing really changes, that the appearance of change masks the world's basic sameness (Fagan 2013). The tragic finale is the re-establishment of the status quo (Gurland-Baker 2013). The "ending" is not really an ending because, while narrative threads are tied up, nothing has really ended; instead, a new generation rises to replace the old and everything continues relatively unchanged (Williams 2014).

## Methodology

This study utilizes textual analysis, which can be used as "a means of trying to learn something about people by examining what they ... produce on television" (Berger 1998, 23). The value of employing textual analysis is that "media texts present a distinctive discursive moment between encoding and decoding that justifies special scholarly engagement" (Fürsich 2009, 238). Meanings from manifest content are socially produced or constructed (Lester-Roushanzamir and Raman 1999). For this textual analysis, the researcher focused on narrative aspects of *The Wire* (Miller 2010). Narratives encourage people to make decisions about aspects of a television program, and an analysis of narrative also allows researchers to make decisions about the artifact they are consuming (Foss 2009). In addition to spoken text, visual features such as type of shot, content, sequencing, and graphics also were analyzed (Foss 2009). In a textual analysis, researchers not only examine the surface content of a program but also aim to unearth all possible meanings (Larsen 1991).

Textual analysis "proceeds from a long soak in the material to an extremely close reading of a specific text as defined by the researcher" (Lester-Roushanzamir and Raman 1999, 703). In this study, the unit of analysis was the spoken and visual text of 60 episodes of *The Wire* that aired on HBO from June 2, 2002, to March 9, 2008. Because of the importance of plot and character development in *The Wire*, the researcher first should clarify the sample. Systematically, each of the 60 episodes of the series, or about 70 hours, was viewed to put the episodes into context. Each episode then was closely analyzed for dialogue, facial expressions, camera framing, lighting, body language, or any other characteristic that could cause the viewer to see a character or situation in a certain manner.

Texts were examined several times: themes emerged during initial viewings and more viewings were conducted to explore those themes (McKee 2003). While coding themes and patterns, the researcher isolated something "(a) that happen[ed] a number of times and (b) that consistently happen[ed] in a specific way" (Miles and Huberman 1984, 215). Thick description is used to determine what those structures of meaning are and to digest their meaning (Geertz 1973). Textual analysis goes beyond the manifest content of messages, allowing researchers to discern "implicit patterns, assumptions and omissions of a text" (Fürsich 2009, 241). Text should be thought of as "an indeterminate field of meaning in which intentions and possible effects intersect. The task of the analysis is to bring out the whole range of possible meanings" (Larsen 1991, 122). Readings have preferred narratives and subjects (Lester-Roushanzamir and Raman 1999). Researchers do agree that multiple readings are possible, and that the author of a text might not have intended what the researcher found in his or her reading of the text (Lester-Roushanzamir and Raman 1999). However, researchers do assume that patterns of values, attitudes, and behavior found in the text reflect and affect those who created it (Berger 1998).

## Findings

The Baltimore depicted in *The Wire* is a failing city. That failure results from the failures of five necessary institutions: the police and justice system, unions and industrial jobs, politicians and the government, the educational system, and the daily newspaper. Each of these institutions will be discussed in more depth.

### *Police and Justice System*

Season 1 centers on the interaction between Baltimore police and a West Baltimore drug gang. Three narcotics detectives, Kima Greggs, Thomas "Herc" Hauk, and Ellis Carver, discuss the futility of the "war on drugs" in Season 1, Episode 1, "The Target":

**Carver:** (to Kima) Girl, you can't even call this shit a war.

**Hauk:** Why not?

**Carver:** Wars end.

However, this war, though futile, shows no signs of ending during the five seasons of *The Wire*. Instead, viewers see failed policies such as street-level drug rips and low-level, quality-of-life policing tried time and again instead of more effective methods such as high-end drug cases and beat policing. The war on drugs also is shown to take a major toll on the officers fighting it. Major "Bunny" Colvin institutes a free drug zone, nicknamed Hamsterdam, during Season 3. In essence, he legalizes drugs in parts of Baltimore. The idea works for a time as crime drops 14 percent in his district, but Colvin ultimately is fired when his scheme is discovered by commanding officers.

The police are shown as failing to stop or even lessen the flow of drugs into West Baltimore. Similarly, the city daily, *The Baltimore Sun*, is shown to fail in adequately covering the war on drugs. Two major stories are missed because *Sun* journalists do not see the connection between an isolated crime and the larger gang wars in West Baltimore. In Season 5, Episode 3, "Not for Attribution," Alma Gutierrez writes about a home invasion that left three people dead. The story, originally slated for the front page, is published in a much shorter version below the fold in Metro. The *Sun* completely misses the murder of a major player in the drug wars, Omar Little. There is space for one brief—either Little's murder or a fire—and the editor decides to run the fire story because he had never heard of Little.

Reporters also are depicted as stenographers instead of watchdog journalists. In Season 5, Episode 4, "Transitions," Gutierrez reports on a press conference where Mayor Thomas Carcetti announces a new interim police commissioner, Bill Rawls. The press conference is broadcast live on television, and editors in the newsroom, especially Gus Haynes, openly mock the "dog-and-pony show." The *Sun* covers the press conference as a straight news story in the next day's paper because there are not enough reporters, especially experienced reporters, to publish real insight into the leadership change. Similarly, in Season 5, Episode 9, "Late Editions," court reporter Bill Zorzi knows that a Carcetti press conference announcing a major drug bust is nothing more than an effort by a failing police department to show that it is doing something to keep the city safe. Viewers see that other news outlets are treating the press conference as major news, suggesting that Zorzi will publish a conventional news story despite his misgivings about the validity of the staged event.

Police on *The Wire* are shown both to fight crime and also to routinely commit criminal acts. Carver, Hauk, Bunk Moreland, Jimmy McNulty, and Roland Pryzbylewski all drive drunk at some point during the series. Detective Michael Santangelo is shown urinating in public. Officer Eddie Walker commits four crimes during Season 4: he steals $200 from a teenager, breaks the fingers of another teenager who had just stolen a car, steals a ring from a suspect, and steals DVDs and T-shirts from a citizen asking for his help. Corrections Officer Dwight Tilghman is depicted smuggling drugs into the prison where he works; he only is arrested after five prisoners die from tainted drugs. Greggs, Carver, Hauk, McNulty, Pryzbylewski, and Lieutenant Cedric Daniels all assault suspects in police custody. Daniels also coaches Pryzbylewski on what to tell internal investigators after the officer assaults a teenager in Season 1, Episode 2, "The Detail," an assault that ultimately causes the teenager to lose his eye:

> **Daniels:** He made you fear for your safety and that of your fellow officers. (Pryzbylewski shakes his head yes.) I'm guessing now, but maybe he was seen to pick up a bottle and menace Officers Hauk and Carver, both of whom had already sustained injury from flying projectiles. Rather than use deadly force in such a situation, maybe you elected to approach the youth, ordering him to drop the bottle. Maybe when he raised the bottle in a threatening manner, you used a KAL light, not the handle of your service weapon, to incapacitate the suspect. (Pryzbylewski shakes his head yes.) Go practice.

The overarching justice system in Baltimore also is shown to be deficient if not outright broken. For example, a local drug gang is shown to intimidate witnesses into changing testimony during Season 1, Episode 1, "The Target." Similarly, several witnesses are murdered before they testify, and another witness is murdered after he testifies. In Season 2, Episode 6, "All Prologue," Assistant State's Attorney Ilene Nathan puts Omar Little, a man who robs drug dealers and whom Nathan knows is lying, on the witness stand to testify against a gang member on trial for murder. While on the stand, Little is cross-examined by Maurice Levy, a Baltimore attorney who makes his career representing drug gangs. He also is a powerful and connected Baltimore attorney, so no other lawyer challenges him in court.

The *Sun* likewise is deficient in covering the court system. For example, in Season 5, Episode 4, "Transitions," no *Sun* reporter is there to cover State Senator Clay Davis leaving the federal courthouse after he gives grand jury testimony. Bill Zorzi, who covers federal courts for the *Sun*, is told to also cover city courts temporarily. He confronts Perlman when State's Attorney Rupert Bond announces Davis' indictment by the grand jury, asking why the prosecutor would stage a perp walk without telling the daily paper. Perlman responds that she left a voicemail for Gail Gibson, the *Sun*'s city court reporter who had left the paper in a round of buyouts four months earlier.

### *Unions and the Loss of Industrial Jobs*

The betrayal and disappearance of the blue-collar working class is shown through three members of the Sobotka family—patriarch Frank, his nephew Nick, and his son

Ziggy. Frank Sobotka is the head of the local dockworkers union, and he is using money collected from illegally importing drugs and stolen goods, as well as human trafficking, to lobby state politicians to reinvest in a canal and grain pier. Without those investments, the docks are dead. As is, most people work one or two days at best.

The union comes under police scrutiny after dock officer Beadie Russell finds 13 dead women in a "can." Police, holding grand jury subpoenas, confront Sobotka during Season 2, Episode 5, "Undertow":

> **Sobotka:** What you're forgetting, detective, is that every IBS [International Brotherhood of Stevedores] local on the East Coast has had its ass in front of a federal grand jury two or three times already. You want to throw your summonses? Throw them. You want to subpoena our records? Shit, you don't even need a subpoena no more. Our books were open to the Justice Department for eight years. We're here through Bobby Kennedy, Tricky Dick Nixon, Ronnie "The Union Buster" Reagan, and half a dozen other sons of bitches. We'll be here through your weak bullshit, no problem.

Season 2 ends with the literal and figurative death of the union. Frank Sobotka is murdered by the "Greeks," the gang for which he was illegally importing women, drugs, and stolen goods. The union itself is decertified by the Federal Bureau of Investigation. The canal will not get dredged because politicians run scared following arrests of union members, and the grain pier is slated to be turned into high-end condos. Frank Sobotka sums up the problem with white-collar betrayal of blue-collar workers during an argument with union lobbyist Bruce DiBiago in Season 2, Episode 2, "Collateral Damage":

> **Sobotka:** You know what the trouble is, Brucie? We used to make shit in this country. Build shit. Now we just put our hand in the next guy's pocket.

Media is virtually nonexistent throughout Season 2. The reason could be that the death of blue-collar jobs in Baltimore is so commonplace that it no longer is newsworthy, or that there has been so many buyouts at *The Baltimore Sun* that there are not enough reporters left to dedicate one to the continued loss of industry. Either way, the continued decline of the dockworkers, and their continued illegal activities on the docks, does not find its way into the daily paper.

### *Politicians and the Government*

City government is shown throughout Season 3 to be at worst corrupt and at best inept. For example, Dennis "Cutty" Wise, a former gang member and convict, is trying to turn his life around by starting a boxing gym for at-risk youth. In Season 3, Episode 9, "Slapstick," Cutty is shown bouncing from one bureaucratic nightmare to another while trying to get the proper permits for his gym.

Corruption is rampant throughout the government. Mayor Clarence Royce funds political campaigns in part through laundered drug money, receives oral sex from his secretary in his office, and uses city employees to harass a political opponent. Major Colvin is practically forced into creating Hamsterdam, his legalized drug zone, from the pressure by police leadership and City Hall to reduce crime rates. State Senator Clay Davis launders drug money for himself and other politicians. He also defrauds Stringer Bell, a notorious drug lord, throughout Season 3. Davis tells Bell that he will take Bell's money to bribe government officials for city, state, and federal contracts, as well as building permits; however, he just pockets the money for himself. *Sun* editor Gus Haynes discovers a shady land deal in a reporter's City Council story; in the deal, the city will buy property from a known drug criminal, "Fat Face Rick" Hendrix for $1.2 million, and then sell him better property for $200,000. *Sun* journalists also find that Hendrix contributed at least $40,000 to Council President Nerese Campbell's campaign fund.

Councilman Thomas Carcetti is positioned as the great hope for reform. He gives a stirring speech during a Council meeting in Season 3, Episode 12, "Mission Accomplished" about the results of corrupt and inept governments:

**Carcetti:** If this disaster demands anything of us as a city, it demands that we say enough. Enough to the despair which makes policemen even think about another surrender. Enough to the fact that these neighborhoods are not saved or are beyond the saving. Enough to this administration's indecisiveness and lethargy, to the garbage which goes uncollected, the lots and row houses which stay vacant, the addicts who go untreated, the working men and women who every day are denied a chance at economic freedom. Enough to the crime, which every day chokes more and more of the life from our city. And the thing of it is, if we don't take responsibility and step up, not just for the mistakes and the miscues, but for whether or not we're going to win this battle for our streets, if that doesn't happen, we're going to lose these neighborhoods and ultimately this city forever.

Carcetti eventually wins the mayoral election; however, viewers soon learn that he is not committed to Baltimore, only to his own political ambitions to run for Maryland governor in two years. Carcetti tells his staff that the "*Sun* papers made us look bad" in Season 5, Episode 2, "Unconfirmed Reports," referring to reportage about city crime rates while he is thinking about a gubernatorial campaign. Carcetti even is willing to shortchange the citizens of Baltimore if hurting them would help his own career. He learns of a $54 million school budget shortfall and must ask the Republican governor for bailout money. However, the governor, knowing that Carcetti is planning to run against him, puts strings on the money that would hurt Carcetti in a statewide election, so Carcetti ultimately turns down the money.

### *Educational System*

Viewers are led into the education system through Pryzbylewski, who they first saw as a police officer in Season 1. Now, he has left the police force to become a teacher. He meets with Tilghman Middle School Principal Claudell Withers and Assistant Principal Marcia Donnelly in Season 4, Episode 1, "Boys of Summer," about a teaching job in mathematics. The administrators are very reluctant to offer a job because Pryzbylewski has not completed the teaching certificate program, but they become much more welcoming when they learn that he used to be a police officer. Pryzbylewski has early struggles as a teacher, getting overwhelmed by students during homeroom, class, and detention. However, he soon becomes one of the best teachers in the school, using a dice game to teach probabilities and statistics, finding new textbooks in the school's storage room, and introducing his students to an unused school computer.

However, he also quickly learns that the school district faces many of the same bureaucratic problems as the police force. This realization comes to a head during a conversation with Rachel Shapiro in the school's teacher's lounge during Season 4, Episode 8, "Corner Boys":

**Shapiro:** Look, you teach math, you teach the test. North Avenue is all about the leave-no-child-behind stuff getting spoon-fed.

**Pryzbylewski:** And what do they learn?

District officials want a 10 percent rise in standardized test scores, so every teacher, no matter what subject they normally teach, is required to change curriculum to focus on mathematics and language skills, emphasizing questions that have been on previous statewide tests. The changes work, at least for the school. Test grades do rise, although the students do not really learn anything. Pryzbylewski learns the truth when speaking with Grace Sampson in Season 4, Episode 13, "Final Grades":

**Sampson:** You believe the numbers?

**Pryzbylewski:** Thirty-eight percent proficient. Eight percent advanced.

**Sampson:** Proficient means they're at least two grades below their level. Advanced can mean they're at grade level or a year below. They score them like that, and they say we're making progress.

*Sun* journalists are interested in publishing a series on how the school system is failing Baltimore children. In Season 5, Episode 2, "Unconfirmed Reports," however, viewers learn that editor James Whiting is more interested in winning a Pulitzer Prize than exposing flaws in the system. Haynes argues that the story must include context, that the problem is systemic and not just confined to a classroom. Whiting counters that the reporting needs to be limited in scope so it does not become "some amorphous series detailing society's ills." Whiting's point is that the Pulitzer committee, on which he used to sit, will look for a tangible problem and solution that can be measured clearly when discussing prizes.

Pryzbylewski is not the only character on *The Wire* who gets caught up in bureaucratic games. Dennis Wise gets a "custodial" job with the school. The job, however, really is a two-month truancy officer position. The school gets a certain amount of money for each child who attends one day in September and one day in October; afterwards, the school does not lose money, so the truancy job is complete. Wise decides to leave the position because he really is not helping kids by forcing them to come to school for only two days. University of Maryland professor David Parenti also gets trapped in bureaucratic games. He convinces school officials to let him implement a pilot program with smaller class sizes and a special curriculum for at-risk youth, the "corner boys" who do not take school seriously and who disrupt their regular classes. The program does have limited success socializing and educating these students, but it is shut down by district administrators and the mayor's office because the students are not being taught the statewide test curriculum. *Sun* reporters also run into bureaucracy when Whiting kills a story about the University of Maryland failing to meet its diversity goals. The paper has a potential story that illustrates racial issues on campus, but Whiting "had lunch" with the dean of journalism, who told him everything is getting much better despite the numbers.

### *The Daily Paper*

*The Baltimore Sun*, the fictional city daily depicted in Season 5, is a failing newspaper. One major problem is a journalistic culture that places profits above good journalism. This mentality in shown in Season 5, Episode 3, "Not for Attribution," when Whiting addresses newsroom staff about the current state of the newspaper industry:

**Whiting:** It's a bad time for newspapers, as you all know. The news hole is shrinking as advertising dollars continue to decline. Our circulation numbers are also down as we compete with a variety of media. Technology is driving distribution, and the internet is a free source of news and opinions. Seeking a balance in this new world, we're now faced with hard choices. We opened our first foreign bureau in London in 1924. The *Sun*'s foreign coverage has been a source of pride ever since. So it is with tremendous regret that I tell you that Chicago has made it clear that bureaus in Beijing, Moscow, Jerusalem, Johannesburg, and London will all be shuttered. Elsewhere in the newsroom, there will be a fresh round of buyouts. Chicago has given us some hard budgetary numbers that will force us into some hard decisions throughout the newsroom. We are quite simply going to have to find ways to do more with less.

Haynes, the city editor who is the exemplar of good journalism, asks why there are such drastic cuts in the newsroom while the paper is profitable. The simple truth is that it is more cost efficient to run an inferior newspaper for less money.

Older reporters are getting fired, and reporters such as Scott Templeton are looking to cut corners, win a prize, and move to a larger paper. Templeton unsuccessfully interviews for a job at the *Washington Post* in Season 5, Episode 4, "Transitions," and begins making ethical lapses while covering homeless killings almost immediately upon his return to Baltimore. He sensationalizes news while writing himself into the story. His much bigger transgression is fabricating quotes, as well as entire interactions with a possible, albeit fake, serial killer. Templeton's transgressions come to a head in Season 5, Episode 10, "-30-" during an interaction between Haynes and Managing Editor Thomas Klebanow:

**Klebanow:** Are you suggesting that Scott made any of this up?

**Haynes:** (Sighs and rubs his head) You ever notice that the guys who do that, the Blairs, the Glasses, the Kelleys, they always start with something small, just a little quote that they clean up. But then it's a whole anecdote, and pretty soon they're seeing some amazing shit. They're the lucky ones who just happen to be standing on the right street corner in Tel Aviv when the pizza joint blows up, and the human head rolls down the street with the eyes still blinking.

**Klebanow:** Gus, this has gotten personal between you and Scott, and it's affecting your judgment. I'm moving the story through the state desk. You should go home. Think this through. We'll talk in the morning.

**Gus:** (Walking out) Maybe you win a Pulitzer with this stuff, and maybe you've got to give it back.

Templeton's homeless killing series—which, again, is largely faked—takes away the paper's ever-shrinking resources and ability to cover more important stories such as the city's gangs, the police and criminal justice system, the loss of industrial jobs, and corruption in politics.

## Conclusions

Communitarianism is based on the premise that there must be a balance between individual autonomy and rights, on one hand, and social responsibilities as they relate to the larger good of a community, on the other. Individuals need interconnected and social cohesion, need to reduce their fragmented lives by broadening their social world to include places and institutions where they can connect and interact with others. However, that premise only works if there is a larger community to be part of. That larger community is broken to the point of nonexistence in *The Wire*. As Carcetti says in Season 4, "We're going to lose these neighborhoods and ultimately this city forever."

The city of Baltimore depicted in *The Wire* is failing because its institutions are failing. Police are losing the war on drugs to West Baltimore gangs in Season 1 because of ineffective police tactics, a prioritization on collecting arrest statistics instead of making meaningful criminal cases, and a broken court system where witnesses routinely are intimidated and murdered and where corrupt lawyers are immune to scrutiny because of their positions within the state bar. A dying union underscores the death of the blue-collar working class in Season 2. Only the most senior union members routinely get a day's work, leaving some younger unionists to start smuggling and stealing in order to earn a day's wage. The union itself is corrupt, smuggling drugs, stolen goods, and women for a local gang. An inept city government results from corrupt Mayor Clarence Royce, who uses laundered drug money to fund his campaign, city employees to harass a political opponent, and his position as mayor to procure sex. Royce's successor, Tommy Carcetti, is shown as the "Great White Hope," but he ultimately sells out the city in favor of his own political career. A failing school system is depicted in Season 4. Students are shoved into overcrowded, unruly classrooms where teachers use outdated books and teach to a statewide test. While some teaching innovations work, district officials are more concerned with increasing statewide test scores than truly educating students. A newspaper doing "less with less" following another round of staff cuts is shown throughout Season 5. The remaining journalists cannot adequately report the failures of institutions seen in previous seasons. Instead, a young reporter is enabled to sensationalize and fabricate stories because head editors sense his series on a homeless serial killer could win a Pulitzer Prize, which could be their ticket to a larger, more secure paper.

*The Wire* shows communitarian failure in institutions, and this failure is significant to journalism and journalism studies in two primary ways. First, news organizations are part of a community and function properly as one part of a larger institutional ecosystem; the press only makes sense in terms of the public and public life (Christians et al. 2009; Dewey 1954). If media fail their normative role to be socially responsible in terms of justice, covenant, and empowerment, then the society in which they operate most likely also will be failing. Similarly, if the social, cultural, legal, political, and economic systems are failing, then the media will not be able (or as able) to fulfill their role in society.

Second, communitarians argue that the ultimate goal of a socially responsible press is to provide citizens with information necessary for self-governance and social transformation. The nature of the public in a communitarian ideal is for individuals to identify as citizens and undertake the obligations of citizenship, namely to engage in political discourse. A necessary component of this political discourse is knowledge of public affairs. Media can and often do provide this needed service in exchange for the community's tacit agreement to compensate them for these services and recognize the right to perform them (Gardner, Csikszentmihalyi, and Damon 2002). However, the breakdown of community, both the Baltimore depicted in *The Wire* and real communities throughout the United States, means that both compensation for services provided and recognition of the right to perform services has been lacking.

The breakdown of community has negatively impacted real-world journalism. There are about 40 percent fewer newsroom employees than there were 20 years ago, and more than 125 daily newspapers folded from 2004 to 2014 (Pew Research Center 2016). Industry consolidation means fewer locally owned newspapers (Pew Research Center 2016), which could mean a scarcity of diverse viewpoints, a lack of local editorial control, and an inability to adequately serve local communities. *The Baltimore Sun* depicted in *The Wire* is owned by Tribune Publishing (now Tronc, Inc.), which institutes a round of newsroom layoffs during Season 5 while the paper is profitable. The message is that the company's bottom line is more important than serving the self-governing informational needs of Baltimore citizens.

Community in *The Wire* is broken because institutions have harmed both the individuals who comprise them and the communities they are meant to serve (Crosby 2013). This depiction is not benign, and it is not unusual. Despite a wealth of coverage, the *Flint Journal* ultimately did not succeed in warning stakeholders about an impending crisis because those citizens, institutions, and communities did not care. There was a total breakdown of the community, a necessary component of any fully functioning media system. Previous literature on the normative role of journalists generally has focused on what journalists owe community stakeholders. However, those community stakeholders also owe duty to journalists. A socially responsible press can only survive as part of a larger community. Therefore, individual citizens and government and non-government institutions must recognize the need for a strong community from which the press can operate to report, explain, correct, and connect.

## DISCLOSURE STATEMENT

No potential conflict of interest was reported by the author.

## REFERENCES

Alvarez, Rafael. 2009. *The Wire: Truth Be Told*. New York, NY: Grove Press.

Anderson, Benedict. 2006. *Imagined Communities: Reflections on the Origin and Spread of Nationalism*. New York, NY: Verso.

Anderson, Rob, Robert Dardenne, and George M. Killenberg. 1997. "The American Newspaper as the Public Conversational Commons." In *Mixed News: The Public/Civic/Communitarian Journalism Debate*, edited by Jay Black, 96–117. Mahway, NJ: Lawrence Erlbaum Associates.

Bell, Daniel. 1993. *Communitarianism and Its Critics*. Oxford: Carendon Press.

Berger, Arthur A. 1998. *Media Research Techniques*. Thousand Oaks, CA: Sage.

Berlin, Isaiah. 2002. *Liberty: Incorporating Four Essays on Liberty*. Oxford: Oxford University Press.

Carey, James W. 1997. "Community, Public, and Journalism." In *Mixed News: The Public/Civic/Communitarian Journalism Debate*, edited by Jay Black, 1–17. Mahway, NJ: Lawrence Erlbaum Associates.

Christians, Clifford G., John P. Ferré, and P. Mark Fackler. 1993. *Good News: Social Ethics and the Press*. Oxford: Oxford University Press.

Christians, Clifford G., Theodore L. Glasser, Denis McQuail, Kaarle Nordenstreng, and Robert A. White. 2009. *Normative Theories of the Media: Journalism in Democratic Societies*. Urbana, IL: University of Illinois Press.

Coleman, Renita, Paul Lieber, Andrew L. Mendelson, and David D. Kurpius. 2008. "Public Life and the Internet: If You Build a Better Website, Will Citizens Become Engaged?" *New Media and Society* 10 (2): 179–201.

Crosby, Joanna. 2013. "This Ain't Aruba, Bitch." In *The Wire and Philosophy*, edited by David Bzdak, Joanna Crosby, and Seth Vannatta, 3–12. Chicago, IL: Open Court.

Culbertson, Hugh M., and Ni Chen. 1997. "Communitarianism: A Foundation for Communication Symmetry." *Public Relations Quarterly* 42 (2): 36–41.

Delaney, Cornelius F. 1994. *The Liberalism-Communitarianism Debate: Liberty and Community Values*. Lanham, MD: Rowman & Littlefield Publishers.

Dewey, John. 1954. *The Public and Its Problems*. Chicago, IL: Swallow Press.

Dewey, John. 1985. *The Later Works, 1925–1953, Vol. 7*. Carbondale, IL: Southern Illinois University Press.

Etzioni, Amitai. 1993. *The Spirit of Community: The Reinvention of American Society*. New York, NY: Touchstone.

Fagan, Ty. 2013. "All in the Game." In *The Wire and Philosophy*, edited by David Bzdak, Joanna Crosby, and Seth Vannatta, 13–30. Chicago, IL: Open Court.

Ferré, John P. 1988. "The Dubious Heritage of Media Ethics: Cause-and-Effect Criticism in the 1890s." *American Journalism* 5 (4): 191–203.

Ferrucci, Pat, and Chad Painter. 2014. "Pseudo Newsgathering: Analyzing Journalists' Use of Pseudo-Events on *The Wire*." *The Image of the Journalist in Popular Culture* 5: 135–169.

Fisher, Kenn. 2013. "The Best of Boys and Lads." In *The Wire and Philosophy*, edited by David Bzdak, Joanna Crosby, and Seth Vannatta, 123–138. Chicago, IL: Open Court.

Foss, Sonja K. 2009. *Rhetorical Criticism: Exploration and Practice*. Long Grove, IL: Waveland Press.

Fürsich, Elfriede. 2009. "In Defense of Textual Analysis." *Journalism Studies* 10 (2): 238–252.

Gardner, Howard E., Mihaly Csikszentmihalyi, and William Damon. 2002. *Good Work: When Excellence and Ethics Meet*. New York, NY: Basics Books.

Geertz, Clifford. 1973. *The Interpretation of Cultures*. New York, NY: Basic Books.

Glasser, Theodore L., and Stephanie Craft. 1997. "Public Journalism and the Prospects for Press Accountability." In *Mixed News: The Public/Civic/Communitarian Journalism Debate*, edited by Jay Black, 120–137. Mahway, NJ: Lawrence Erlbaum Associates.

Gurland-Baker, Avram. 2013. "*The Wire* as American Tragedy." In *The Wire and Philosophy*, edited by David Bzdak, Joanna Crosby, and Seth Vannatta, 193–204. Chicago, IL: Open Court.

Guttman, Nurit. 2007. "Bringing the Mountain to the Public: Dilemmas and Contradictions in the Procedures of Public Deliberation Initiatives That Aim to Get 'Ordinary Citizens' to Deliberate Policy Issues." *Communication Theory* 17 (4): 411–438.

Habermas, Jürgen. 1991. *The Structural Transformation of the Public Sphere: An Inquiry Into a Category of Bourgeois Society*. Boston, MA: MIT Press.

Hallin, Daniel C., and Paolo Mancini. 2004. *Comparing Media Systems: Three Models of Media and Politics*. Cambridge: Cambridge University Press.

Hanson, Christopher. 2008. "Some Last Words on *The Wire*." *Film Quarterly* 62 (2): 66–67.

Herbert, Daniel. 2012. "It Is What It Is: *The Wire* and the Politics of Anti-Allegorical Television Drama." *Quarterly Review of Film & Video* 29 (3): 191–202.

Hiner, John. 2016. "Letter to the Editor: Local Media Didn't Whiff on Flint Coverage." http://www.poynter.org/2016/letter-to-the-editor-national-not-local-media-whiffed-on-flint-coverage/393583/.

Hodges, Louis W. 1997. "Ruminations About the Communitarian Debate." In *Mixed News: The Public/Civic/Communitarian Journalism Debate*, edited by Jay Black, 38–51. Mahway, NJ: Lawrence Erlbaum Associates.

Larsen, Peter. 1991. "Textual Analysis of Fictional Media Content." In *A Handbook of Qualitative Methodologies for Mass Communication Research*, edited by Klaus Bruhn Jensen and Nicholas W. Jankowski, 121–134. New York, NY: Routledge.

Lester-Roushanzamir, Elli P., and Usha Raman. 1999. "The Global Village in Atlanta: A Textual Analysis of Olympic News Coverage for Children in the *Atlanta Journal-Constitution*." *Journalism and Mass Communication Quarterly* 76 (4): 699–712.

McChesney, Robert W. 1999. *Rich Media, Poor Democracy: Communication Politics in Dubious Times*. Champaign, IL: University of Illinois Press.

McKee, Alan. 2003. *Textual Analysis: A Beginner's Guide*. Thousand Oaks, CA: Sage.

Miles, Matthew, and A. Michael Huberman. 1984. *Qualitative Data Analysis: A Sourcebook of New Methods*. Thousand Oaks, CA: Sage.

Miller, Toby. 2010. *Television Studies: The Basics*. New York, NY: Routledge.

Mutz, Diana C., and Paul S. Martin. 2001. "Facilitating Communication Across Lines of Political Differences and the Role of Mass Media." *American Political Science Review* 95 (1): 97–115.

Nerone, John C. 1995. *Last Rights: Revisiting Four Theories of the Press*. Urbana, IL: University of Illinois Press.

O'Rourke, Meghan. 2006. "Behind *The Wire*." http://www.slate.com/id/2154694/.

Pew Research Center. 2016. "Newspapers: Fact Sheet." http://www.journalism.org/2016/06/15/newspapers-fact-sheet/.

Postman, Neil. 1985. *Amusing Ourselves to Death: Public Discourse in the Age of Show Business*. New York, NY: Penguin Books.

Putnam, Robert D. 2000. *Bowling Alone: The Collapse and Revival of American Community*. New York, NY: Simon & Schuster.

Sabin, Roger. 2011. "*The Wire*: Dramatising the Crisis in Journalism." *Journalism Studies* 12 (2): 139–155.

Sandel, Michael J. 1996. *Democracy's Discontent: America in Search of a Public Philosophy*. Cambridge, MA: Harvard University Press.

Schaub, Joseph C. 2010. "*The Wire*: Big Brother is Not Watching You in Body-more, Murdaland." *Journal of Popular Film & Television* 38 (3): 122–132.

Simon, David. 2009. "Introduction." In *The Wire: Truth Be Told*, edited by Rafael Alvarez, 1–31. New York, NY: Grove Press.

Smith, Jeffrey A. 1988. *Printers and Press Freedom: The Ideology of Early American Journalism*. Oxford: Oxford University Press.

Steiner, Linda. 2013. "*The Wire* and Repair of the Journalistic Paradigm." *Journalism* 14 (6): 703–720.

Tam, Henry. 1998. *Communitarianism: A New Agenda for Politics and Citizenship*. New York, NY: New York University Press.

The Commission on Freedom of the Press. 1947. *A Free and Responsible Press*. Chicago, IL: The University of Chicago Press.

Williams, Linda. 2014. *On The Wire*. Durham, NC: Duke University Press.

Zizek, Slavoj. 2013. "*The Wire*, or, What to do in Non-Evental Times." In *The Wire and Philosophy*, edited by David Bzdak, Joanna Crosby, and Seth Vannatta, 217–236. Chicago, IL: Open Court.

# WHAT DOES SOCIETY OWE POLITICAL CARTOONISTS?

**Jenn Burleson Mackay**

*Political cartoonists challenge the government, question societal norms, and contribute to public discussion. They may show the public instances of injustice and help society to understand our own roles and responsibilities within the community. Yet, cartoonists are facing significant challenges in modern society. As the newspaper industry has struggled financially, fewer news organizations have continued to maintain a staff cartoonist. The shootings at France's satirical newspaper* Charlie Hebdo *served as a reminder of the dangers that cartoonists can face if they publish controversial cartoons. Through applications of John Rawls' political liberalism and communitarianism, this paper examines what cartoonists contribute to societal justice and their role in the community. It argues that society owes cartoonists the liberties that they need to continue upholding justice, but that cartoonists have responsibilities to the community.*

## Introduction

Political cartoonists question government policies and mock popular culture. They utilize artistic prowess as a tool to comment on societal flaws. They are journalists who provide the public news and information. Yet they challenge audiences in a unique way. They ask the public to see the irony embedded within current events. They interpret the news and show us a perspective that the audience may or may not be prepared to accept. They are storytellers, chroniclers of history, critics, and artists.

Political cartoons have the ability to change people's opinions (Neuberger and Kremar 2008). Harrison (1981, 31) describes a cartoon as "educator and editorialist, as seller and seducer." Cartoonists and editorial page editors feel that political cartoons provoke thought. They also can advocate change and be entertaining (Ammons, King, and Yeric 1988, 84). Yet cartoonists have a responsibility to act as critics (Riffe, Sneed, and Van Ommeren 1985). Those advocacy and critic functions help separate them from rank and file journalists. They allow cartoonists to challenge the government and empower ordinary people. Cartoonists concisely add thoughtful ideas to the conversation in a way that traditional journalists, who are constrained by the expectations of objectivity, cannot. As a result, political cartoonists contribute to the public deliberation of issues.

New technology has allowed global information sharing and has empowered billions of voices. While language barriers can stand in the way of sharing information to a global audience, visual communication can transcend those barriers (Müller, Özcan, and Scizov 2009). Anyone can post their opinions across social media sites regardless of whether they are well-informed or well-intentioned. Misinformation runs rampant. The most talented political cartoonists have the ability to step into that fray and communicate a brief yet thoughtful message that is derived from careful observation and understanding of issues.

Yet, the profession has come under attack during the past few years. Cartoonists in some countries have been arrested for publishing cartoons that offended authoritarian governments. Iranian cartoonist Nikahang Kowsar was charged with "undermining national security" after he drew a cartoon in 2000 of a reporter being choked by a reptile, whose name rhymed with the nickname of an Iranian cleric. South African cartoonist Zapiro received death threats after he drew a cartoon in 2010 of the Prophet Muhammad. While new technology has created new publishing opportunities for cartoonists and the possibility of escape from some censorship, it also has created problems. Cartoonist Rebel Pepper jumped from one social media site to another as the Chinese government shut down the accounts where he published his cartoons. The cartoonist, who eventually moved to Japan, has suggested that some of his audience members were questioned by the police because they shared his cartoons (Guyer 2015).

Most recently, cartoonists have found themselves at the center of a religious controversy with the shootings at France's satirical newspaper *Charlie Hebdo*. The cause of the shootings largely was blamed on the newspaper's publication of cartoons that satirized Islam and the Prophet Muhammad. Political cartoonists were among the 17 people killed (Higgins and Bilefsky 2015). Cartoonists across the globe responded to the shootings with their own images of grief and anger. Some cartoons depicted pens fending off terrorists or cartoonists under attack, while others illustrated cartoonists holding up their pencils in solidarity.

The *Charlie Hebdo* controversy was reminiscent of a prior Muslim cartoon debate that erupted after Denmark's newspaper *Jyllands-Posten* published a series of cartoons depicting the Prophet Muhammad. Protests erupted around the world after newspapers in other countries republished the images (Cowell 2006). What some people saw as an exercise in freedom of speech, others saw as offensive mockery.

Cartoonists also have struggled from the changing economic state of the newspaper industry. Few newspapers continue to employ an editorial cartoonist. Instead, they prefer to purchase less-expensive cartoons through syndication. As a result, entrepreneurship has become imperative to the economic survival of the political cartoonist. A study from the Herb Block Foundation found that many cartoonists lack health insurance or pension plans. Likewise, the cartoonist's job has changed dramatically. They have become more dependent on social media and new technologies. Some employers even require cartoonists to animate cartoons (Herb Block Foundation 2011).

While the political cartoonist's world is changing dramatically, the value of their content remains unchanged. Political cartoonists publicize and question the government to keep justice in check. They help readers to question societal norms in the pursuit of justice. They can publicize new regulations and question their constitutionality. Cartoonists can help their audience to recognize infringements on their own liberties or the rights of others. Likewise, cartoonists can reconnect readers to their communities. They can help individuals to see their role in the community and recognize their responsibilities to society.

Using two distinct approaches to ethics, this paper will consider what society owes this group of people who can ignite laughter or anger with a few strokes of a pen. First, it describes John Rawls' theory of justice and his arguments for political liberalism. Then, it examines the communitarian perspective and importance of balancing individual rights with responsibilities to the community. It explores the role that cartoonists play in maintaining a just society by exposing inequalities and reminding the citizens of their own rights, while also evaluating the duty that cartoonists have in solidifying shared community values. While relying on examples from political cartoons published in the United States, this paper argues that society owes political cartoonists the freedom to publish critical cartoons and the opportunity to focus on controversial issues, but that the cartoonists must recognize and uphold the responsibilities that come with those rights.

## John Rawls and Justice

Rawls published his theory of justice as an alternative to utilitarianism in 1972. The theory evolved to place more emphasis on stability and a political conception of justice. In *Political Liberalism*, the philosopher argues that stability can exist through the public financing of elections, equal opportunity, a "decent distribution of income and wealth," employment, and health care (Rawls 1996, lix). Rawls argues that a just society must recognize and embrace reasonable pluralism, such as the acceptance of diverse religions. While pluralism can be irrational and angry, reasonable pluralism acknowledges that a variety of rational, comprehensive ideas can be accepted (Rawls 1996). Reasonable people are capable of fairness and understand that disagreements about religion and morality will exist. Unreasonable people, who lack that ability, lose power in Rawls' just society (Friedman 2000).

The theory posits that justice can be achieved if individuals are stripped of their biases behind a hypothetical condition that Rawls calls the veil of ignorance. While individuals are behind the veil, they are tasked with developing the rules for their society. The people behind the veil do not know anything about their society, the people that they are representing, or the concept of good. His revision of the theory suggests that two moral powers are present during this stage: "the capacity for a sense of justice and the capacity for a conception of the good" (Rawls 1996, 5). The moral powers allow social cooperation to exist. In Rawls' eyes, social cooperation is the key to establishing a just society in a pluralistic world. Participants engaged in social cooperation follow coordinated rules, recognize fairness, and embrace an understanding of what every other participant needs. Rawls argues that the state of the veil inevitably will lead the group to accept two specific principles of justice (Rawls 1991).

In the revised version of the theory, the first principle of justice states that:

> Each person has an equal claim to a fully adequate scheme of equal basic rights and liberties, which scheme is compatible with the same scheme for all; and in this scheme the equal political liberties, and only those liberties, are to be guaranteed their fair value. (Rawls 1996, 5)

Rawls suggests that these basic liberties will be accepted because they are to everyone's advantage, they emphasize self-respect, and they lead to a well-ordered society. People in a well-ordered society accept the principles of justice. They agree to the same basic beliefs about human nature, political structures, and social institutions. People agree to these beliefs because they can be supported through public discussion and reasoning (Rawls 1996).

Specific rights are fundamental to the first principle of justice. Maffettone summarizes the rights guaranteed by the first principle as:

- Liberty of religion and conscience;
- Political liberties, including freedom of expression, of the press, of assembly, a vote, and of association;
- Freedom of the person, starting from the inadmissibility of slavery and enslavement and the freedom from physical and psychological oppression, and including also the freedom to hold personal properties and the liberties of movement and of choice of one's occupation;
- Rights and liberties laid down by the "rule of law," like the right to personal freedom, habeas corpus, and the right to a proper administration of justice. (Maffettone 2010, 57)

The second principle of justice is often referred to as the difference principle. This principle focuses on the importance of balancing resources across society. The principle states:

> social and economic inequalities are to satisfy two conditions: first, they are to be attached to positions and offices open to all under conditions of fair equality of opportunity; and second, they are to be to the greatest benefits of the least advantaged members of society. (Rawls 1996, 6)

The difference principle is designed to focus on social goods such as wealth, self-respect, power, and opportunity. Rawls defines the least advantaged in society by using an index that summarizes an individual's social primary goods such as his or her basic liberties, occupational choice, income, and self-respect (Maffettone 2010). Any societal adjustments made by way of the difference principle cannot supersede the rights guaranteed by the first principle of justice. Rawls further suggests that all the rules for the society should be general enough that everyone can understand them and that they should be universally applicable to everyone in society (Rawls 1991).

## The Communitarian Approach

While Rawls focuses on protecting the rights of the individual, communitarianism argues that individual rights must be placed into the context of the community. The communitarian argues that individual rights should be balanced with responsibilities. Community may be defined as neighborhoods, counties, nations, and other geographic areas, but they need not be constrained by geographic boundaries. Those who are part of a community must have a shared set of values (Borden 2014). It is important that people feel that they are part of something. In the words of Culbertson and Chen (1997, 38), "The basic idea here is that members of a community must feel they have something in common that's worth sacrificing for."

Coleman (2000) compares community to a Russian nesting doll where communities are layered on top of other communities.

The communitarian suggests that there is an imbalance in rights versus responsibilities in society. People are quick to fight for the rights of citizens, but, from the communitarian perspective, they fail to acknowledge that responsibilities must accompany rights. Etzioni (1993), one of the pioneers of communitarianism, proposes that this imbalance must be corrected. The first step in correcting the imbalance is to stop establishing new rights. This moratorium should be temporary, but it should allow the community to take time to distinguish between what should be considered a right versus what should be treated as a privilege. Etzioni says that the constant development of new rights devalues other rights. Also, rights should be connected to responsibilities. If one wants the right to a jury of his or her peers, for example, that person also must be willing to serve on a jury rather than look for ways to avoid jury duty. One should not expect to maintain a right if he or she is not willing to uphold the responsibility associated with that right. Third, individuals should accept that some responsibilities, such as the need to care for the environment, do not lead to specific rights. A moral responsibility should not be ignored merely because it is not associated with a specific individual right. Finally, as rights and responsibilities are re-evaluated, some adjustments to existing rights should be made, thus allowing for the elimination of any rights that are weakening the community.

The communitarian perspective suggests that a responsive community should develop a set of moral values that are:

- Nondiscriminatory.
- Easy to understand.
- Based on a common interpretation of justice.
- Not focused on one specific category such as individualism, but rather represent a plethora of values (Etzioni 1993).

Morality is a hallmark of community. One key to establishing a stronger and more moral community is for children to be taught values in school. The communitarian sees these as values that are common throughout society, such as respecting other people. Similarly, the theory heralds the freedom of speech, but unlike more liberal approaches to speech, the communitarian adds that morality is important. Individuals have the right to say what they choose, but that does not mean they *should* say something that is harmful to others (Etzioni 1993).

Admittedly, it is difficult for everyone to agree on a common set of values; nonetheless, it is important for people throughout the community to work together: "Commitment to striving for common ground may be as important as attaining it" (Culbertson and Chen 1997, 39). Being tolerant of those with differing ideas is one attribute of communitarianism. One must be willing to discuss issues. Borden (2014) suggests that hospitality may be preferable to tolerance because it creates an environment of mutuality, where everyone is equal. Hospitality invites discussion and embraces difference. Borden argues that hospitality allows individuals to uphold their own understanding of a common good while also talking with and learning from those who have different perspectives.

Theorists have suggested that a communitarian approach to journalism would lead to a stronger, more socially responsible news media (Christians, Ferré, and Fackler 1993). Borden (2010, 54) goes so far as to suggest that journalism should "help citizens discover the common good as intellectually responsible participants in a diverse political community."

## The Role of the Political Cartoonist

While political cartoonists have different job descriptions from reporters and other employees in the newsroom, the artists view their role in the media similarly to other journalists. As part of a broad study on the ethics of political cartoonists, the author and a colleague administered a survey to 94 political cartoonists, which asked them to assign importance to a series of media roles that traditionally have been applied to journalists.[1] They responded to a seven-level scale that ranged from extremely important to not at all important. The cartoonists most frequently indicated that investigating government claims was extremely important to their jobs. They also stated that providing analysis and interpretation of complex problems, discussing national policies, and providing interpretation of international developments were extremely important. They were less likely to assign a high level of importance to setting the political agenda or, surprisingly, entertainment (Table 1).[2] By fulfilling these roles, political cartoonists help direct readers toward a well-ordered society. They help publicize issues of justice and focus attention on issues of inequality. These roles allow the cartoonist to remind the public of their rights in a just society, as guaranteed by the first principle of justice. They also can draw attention to violations of the difference principle and issues of inequality. These roles also can help in developing a strong community. The communitarian, however, would want to see cartoonists who had a higher interest in motivating individuals to be involved in the community. They also would want to see a higher level of interest in cartoonists helping society to find solutions to problems. While both of these items generally had some degree of importance to most of the survey participants, they clearly were not the most important areas of influence.

As political cartoonists investigate government claims, they call attention to issues where the government may be impeding the rights of specific groups of people. For example, cartoonist Clay Bennett drew a cartoon in response to the state of Tennessee's

**TABLE 1**
Media roles for political cartoonists

| | Importance percentages | | | | | | |
|---|---|---|---|---|---|---|---|
| **Media roles** | **Extremely** | **Very** | **Moderate** | **Neutral** | **Slightly** | **Low** | **No** |
| Investigate government | 71.4 | 22.0 | 2.2 | 2.2 | 1.1 | 1.1 | 0 |
| Provide analysis of complex problems | 60.4 | 28.6 | 3.3 | 5.5 | 0 | 1.1 | 1.1 |
| Discuss national policy | 52.7 | 31.9 | 11.0 | 3.3 | 1.1 | 0 | 0 |
| Provide interpretation of international developments | 49.5 | 30.8 | 11.0 | 5.5 | 1.1 | 2.2 | 0 |
| Get information out quickly | 44 | 31.9 | 20.9 | 2.2 | 0 | 1.1 | 0 |
| Avoid unverified stories | 35.2 | 31.9 | 16.5 | 8.8 | 4.4 | 2.2 | 1.1 |
| Motivate involvement | 33.0 | 33.0 | 25.3 | 4.4 | 2.2 | 0 | 2.2 |
| Point toward possible societal solutions | 26.4 | 37.4 | 14.3 | 11.0 | 4.4 | 3.3 | 3.3 |
| Be skeptical of businesses | 24.2 | 19.8 | 19.8 | 19.8 | 6.6 | 8.8 | 1.1 |
| Allow people to express public affairs views | 19.8 | 36.3 | 25.3 | 3.3 | 6.6 | 6.6 | 2.2 |
| Be skeptical of officials | 22 | 20.9 | 23.1 | 17.6 | 8.8 | 7.7 | 0 |
| Develop intellectual and cultural interests | 24.2 | 20.9 | 28.6 | 8.8 | 5.5 | 5.5 | 6.6 |
| Provide news of widest public interest | 6.6 | 7.7 | 31.9 | 15.4 | 7.7 | 27.5 | 3.3 |
| Set political agenda | 5.5 | 9.9 | 18.7 | 19.8 | 7.7 | 14.3 | 24.2 |
| Entertain | 4.4 | 8.8 | 19.8 | 13.2 | 17.6 | 20.9 | 15.4 |

decision to adopt the Bible as the official state book. The cartoon, titled "The Official Book," depicts a book of matches bearing the words "official book of the state of Tennessee." The burned remnants of the Constitution of the United States surround the matchbook (Bennett 2016). The cartoon suggests that the government has crossed the line separating church and state. It indicates that the government is stepping on the rights of people who do not believe in the Christian Bible and asks people to consider the full ramifications of this governmental decision on the Constitution of the United States. Rawls' first principle of justice suggests that everyone should be free to choose and practice the religion of their choice. No specific doctrine should be forced upon them. Reasonable people, as they are defined by Rawls, should be capable of accepting the notion that people across society have varying religious perspectives. Thus, the cartoonist has drawn attention to an issue that infringes upon Rawls' just society. Rather than focusing on the individual rights, the communitarian would question whether the cartoon was helping society to maintain a set of moral values that supported everyone throughout the community. In this case, the communitarian might suggest that the cartoon is drawing attention to an issue that could discriminate against some members of the community. Therefore, the cartoon is helping to draw attention to a potential threat.

*Washington Post* cartoonist Ann Telnaes, who won the Pulitzer Prize for editorial cartooning in 2001, drew a cartoon in response to Mississippi's Religious Liberty bill. The legislation says that businesses and public employees cannot be punished for refusing services to people when those services are contradictory to their own personal religious beliefs (Kaplan 2016). Telnaes' cartoon depicts a waitress in a diner. A handkerchief that reads "Mississippi" adorns the waitress' uniform. She holds a coffee pot as she says "Have a nice day and God bless." She's standing beside a sign that says "We serve straights only, no LGBT." A short paragraph accompanied the cartoon. The text suggests that Mississippi's bill and the treatment of the LGBT community are similar to the discrimination of blacks before the Civil Rights movement (Telnaes 2016). The cartoon demonstrates Telnaes' desire to interpret a complex problem and to put it into perspective in a large, historic scale. By drawing a comparison between the Mississippi law and the Civil Rights movement, Telnaes' cartoon illustrates the means by which a single law may infringe upon the rights for individuals to be free of physical and psychological oppression, a right that is protected by the first principle of justice. Her association of the new law with the Civil Rights movement echoes with the history of slavery within the United States. Rawls says that in a well-ordered society, everyone has accepted the principles of justice and their acceptance is publicized. Telnaes' cartoon suggests that everyone has not accepted the same set of rights. They have not accepted a common understanding as to human nature. While the communitarian also is opposed to discriminatory practices, he or she might not be as comfortable with this image as Rawls. The cartoon is drawing attention to a problem in the shared moral values within the community, but it is doing so in a potent way, which is likely to lead to argument rather than discussion. This is not the sort of cartoon that may help strengthen the community; rather, it is likely to divide people who already are on separate sides of the issue. Rather than mocking the people of Mississippi, the communitarian would recommend that the cartoonist find a way to illustrate the common values that people have regardless of sexuality. The cartoonist has a right to draw what she wants, but she also has a responsibility to help the community thrive. If the community has lost its path, the cartoonist should try to remind citizens of their moral values and draw them back together. This cartoon not only divides the people within the state of Mississippi. It also separates the people of the state from the nation as a whole.

Similarly, after North Carolina passed a bill that bans people from using bathrooms and locker rooms that do not match their birth certificate-specified gender, Adam Zyglis drew a cartoon for the *Buffalo News* depicting three bathroom doors. One door has a symbol for a male on it. The second door has a symbol for a female on it. The last door has a symbol of a pig on it and the words "N.C. legislators" (Zyglis 2016). This cartoon is publicizing legislation that has not been universally supported. Likewise, it points to a disagreement in society as to what represents human nature. It also might be interpreted to suggest that legislators do not have to follow the same societal expectations as everyone else. They have a door all to themselves, which separates them from the rest of society. Both Telnaes' and Zyglis' cartoons illustrate the cartoonist's role in investigating the government and interpreting problems. They illustrate their perception of a flawed justice system, where society has not accepted the same beliefs in regards to human nature or political structures. Both cartoonists are publicizing what they perceive as societal problems, which are weakening the establishment of a well-ordered society. Yet, from the perspective of the communitarian, both also are drawing images that may further divide the community. Rather than inviting a discussion, these images may lead to unhealthy arguments.

A variety of cartoonists drew cartoons in response to the shootings at *Charlie Hebdo*. Telnaes drew a woman posed as the Statue of Liberty. Rather than holding a torch and a tablet, the woman holds a pencil and a copy of *Charlie Hebdo* (Telnaes 2015). The cover of the magazine shows one of the controversial Islamic cartoons that was published by *Charlie Hebdo* before the shooting occurred. Several other cartoons emphasized freedom. Gary Varvel drew a desk with a sheet of paper reading the word "FREEDOM" in a cartoon for the *Indianapolis Star*. Blood is splattered across the desk and the paper (Varvel 2015). These cartoons illustrate the cartoonist's role in interpreting complex problems and the interpretation of international developments. The cartoons can be interpreted as providing audiences with a reminder of the importance of individual freedom and freedom of the press. These cartoons remind people of one of the fundamental liberties granted by the first principle of justice. They also illustrate a need for an individual to maintain the right to choose his or her own occupation without fear of retribution. They remind viewers that the cartoonist loses the freedom to choose an occupation if he or she is not free to do that job without fear of being murdered. The cartoons call for solidarity across the globe. While the emphasis may be directed as consensus among cartoonists, it might also be interpreted to be a call for society as a whole to unite and accept the idea of the importance of freedom of expression to the political cartoonist. The images suggest that the cartoonist should have the right to publish cartoons, even if those cartoons might be offensive to some people. This form of solidarity supports the concept of Rawls' well-ordered society—a place where everyone accepts the same basic beliefs and embracing freedom of expression. While the communitarian supports freedom of expression, he or she would argument that the cartoonist has an obligation to consider the effects that particular images might have on the community. The communitarian would support images that demonstrated a shared value, freedom, across the globe. They also would support depictions of shared sadness. The communitarian, however, would not be comfortable with an image depicting the Prophet Muhammad. While the shooting at *Charlie Hebdo* would have been condemned in communitarian society, responding to that horrific incident with images known to be offensive would not build a stronger society. They continue to hurt one group of people—Muslims.

Political cartoonists can also call attention to issues where the difference principle has been violated. The water crisis in Flint, Michigan, captured national attention. News reports revealed that people were drinking lead-contaminated water. The problem started after the city chose to stop using Detroit's water treatment plant and began using its own in April 2014. Lead contamination is particularly problematic for young children or pregnant women because it can affect the development of the brain and nervous system (Tanner 2016). *Detroit Free Press* cartoonist Mike Thompson responded to the water problem in Flint with a cartoon that depicted two black children walking through the city. At the top of the cartoon are the words "Report: The U.S. has spent $6 billion in tax dollars on the ISIS problem in the Middle East." The water tower behind them reads "Flint Water." One girl says to the other, "Too bad lead comes out our faucets instead of oil" (Thompson 2015). This cartoon fulfills the cartoonist's roles of analyzing a complex problem and drawing attention to a national policy. The cartoonist questions the government's decision to spend money overseas while serious environmental and health issues exist within the United States. It places particular emphasis on the group of people who are among the most disadvantaged in US society—the children of Flint. According to Rawls, an index is used to determine which people are the least advantaged in society. That index considers items such as power, income, and self-respect. The children of Flint certainly would be among the least advantaged people of the United States. They have been exposed to toxic levels of lead for months. Their families lack the financial means to get themselves out of their situation. It may be impossible to reverse the health problems that they have sustained from their exposure to tainted water. Children, traditionally, do not have a high degree of political or economic power, but certainly the Flint children have less than the average middle-class child of suburban America. Rawls' difference principles suggest that resources should be adjusted to benefit those people who are least advantaged in society. The cartoon suggests that the nation has failed to address the needs of the most disadvantaged people. Instead, money has been redirected toward the Middle East, the land of oil. The cartoon suggests that there is a problematic policy in the well-ordered society. The cartoonist hints that the United States may be fighting ISIS because the nation wants to protect its access to oil in the Middle East. The difference principle suggests that resources need to be redirected to help those who are the least advantaged in society. In this case, the cartoonist suggests that the government has ignored the people who need the most help. The cartoonist is demonstrating the existence of a flawed political structure, which allocates more money overseas to protect natural resources than toward supporting citizens at home. The cartoon also opens up the opportunity for a public discussion that re-examines how money is allocated. The communitarian would see the cartoon as illustrating a community problem. One might suggest that the cartoon is reminding society of a moral duty—the importance of caring for the young in an impoverished community.

Poverty often is a topic addressed by political cartoonists. Cartoonist John Darkow of the *Columbia Daily Tribune* drew a cartoon that focused on poverty shortly after the Census Bureau reported that 46.2 million people were living in poverty. It was the highest number in 52 years (Tavernise 2011). Darkow drew a cartoon with the words, "Poverty level in America reaches 52-year peak!" It showed an enormous man gobbling up multiple pieces of pie. The word "rich" is on a napkin tied around his neck. An empty pie dish labeled "economic pie" sits in front of him along with two small, elderly people with their heads tilted downward. A dialog bubble reads, "You poor folks. Looking at me like that almost makes me feel guilty! You should be ashamed of yourselves" (Darkow 2011). This cartoon draws attention to the discrepancy between the rich and the poor and suggests that the wealthy continually get wealthier while leaving nothing behind for the poor. The physical size of the people within the image draws attention to the imbalance of power between the wealthy and the poor. The language also suggests that the wealthy make light of the problem and try to make the poor feel guilty as the rich keep getting wealthier. Similar to the Flint cartoon, this cartoon depicts an unjust system that favors the most privileged people in society over others, which violates the difference principle. By drawing attention to this problem, Darkow publicizes the belief that there is a problem in political and social structures within the nation. The communitarian likely would agree with the decision to draw a cartoon that focuses on the problem with poverty within the community. Rather than mocking the wealthy, however, they might suggest that the cartoonist draw a cartoon that reminds everyone of their responsibilities to the community. They might focus on ways that the wealthy can support those that may be struggling financially.

Other cartoonists have drawn attention to other economic discrepancies in society. Cartoonist Rob Rogers drew an image depicting the issues with veterans. One two-part cartoon showed a tomb, surrounded by wreaths and human arms holding flowers. The words "The unknown soldiers" are at the top of the image. The second image has the words "The known solider." It shows a man sitting on a sheet of newspaper on the sidewalk. An empty bottle is beside him. In one hand, he holds a tin can. In the other hand he holds a sign reading "homeless, suicidal and suffering from PTSD [post-traumatic stress disorder]." A comment bubble above his head reads "Hello? ... Anyone? ... " A paragraph above the cartoon describes the number of veterans who kill themselves every day and the number of veterans who are homeless and struggling with PTSD (Rogers 2014). The cartoon demonstrates the cartoonist's role in discussing national policies and analyzing problems. It calls attention to veterans' loss of self-respect, poverty, loss of occupation, and lack of power. It shows another violation of the difference principle and calls for change. The cartoon asks people to give the same attention to living soldiers as they do those that are dead and unidentifiable. From the communitarian perspective, the cartoon reminds everyone of their responsibility to the veterans in their community.

The political cartoonist has the ability to remind the public of the rights that everyone deserves in Rawls' just society. They serve important roles in investigating the government and analyzing complex problems throughout society. Like other journalists, they have the ability to publicize information. By illustrating the principles of justice or acts of injustice, cartoonists can give people the information that they need to develop a well-ordered society. The cartoonist's freedom from the journalistic constraints of objectivity allows them to analyze issues and present information that can help the public to understand infringements on their rights. They can draw attention to disparity in society and motivate citizens to discuss important, and perhaps overlooked, issues throughout society. They can stir conversations and debate, which can contribute to societal change. The political cartoonist has a unique opportunity to contribute to a just society.

While the cartoonist focuses on drawing attention to those issues, they can cross a line that damages the community, from the perspective of the communitarian. The role of the cartoonist is not just about reminding people of their individual rights. The cartoonist should look for ways to strengthen the community. They should call attention to problems within society, but they need to illustrate those issues in a way that can help the community rather than divide it. The cartoonist has the right to free speech and the right to publicize issues, but they also have a responsibility to use caution. They should reinforce community values without creating additional tension.

## What Are Political Cartoonists Owed?

While cartoonists help draw attention to the problems of justice within society, they have been the target of death threats and terrorist attacks. Few cartoonists have a job where they are directly associated with a specific newspaper (Herb Block Foundation 2011). Instead, many rely on entrepreneurial opportunities, which may have varying degrees of financial security. Political cartoonists are operating in a world where technology is rapidly changing the way that they do their jobs. If they are not directly affiliated with a news organization, they may have to develop new skills and keep up with new technology without any guidance or support. From the perspective of John Rawls, society surely owes something to the journalists who help ensure the justice of others. That being said, the cartoonist is a member of the community. The communitarian might suggest that the question here should not be what the cartoonist is owed, but rather what the cartoonist owes his or her community. Therefore, if one is to talk about the rights that cartoonists are owned, one also must discuss the obligations that the cartoonist owes the community.

### *New Media Education and Training*

Stability is fundamental to a well-ordered society. Rawls suggests that several "prerequisites" provide the foundation for a society that can support the two principles of justice (Rawls 1996, lix). One of these requirements is equal opportunity. Rawls notes that it is particularly important that opportunities be available in terms of education and training. New media technology has drastically changed the way that political cartoonists do their jobs. This suggests that the cartoonists should receive education to support their ability to publish content online. They should be trained in the use of social media and the development of animated cartoons. If they are required to blog, they should receive training in how to write headlines and other content that are search engine-optimized, and, therefore, more likely to drive traffic to their website. If they are posting cartoons to other social media such as Instagram or Twitter, they should be trained in the use of hashtags and other strategies that will assist them in building an audience. Cartoonists also would benefit from training on the development of a personal brand. The more that they need to rely on entrepreneurial work, the more important it is that they develop a brand for themselves that will give them a reliable online presence. This can help them to build a stronger readership base and potentially help them garner attention from more news organizations. The lack of this training could interfere with the political cartoonist's ability to compete successfully. It places cartoonists at a disadvantage in terms of power. Those people who are better trained in their occupations, who are familiar with concepts such as search engine optimization and personal branding, are going to be able to take advantage of their basic liberties more effectively than those who lack such training.

The communitarian might struggle with the argument that the cartoonist is owed training and educational opportunities. He or she likely sees education as a privilege rather than a right and would question who would pay for the cartoonist's opportunities. To accommodate both Rawls and the communitarian perspective, the best option might be for a system of affordable resources, which likely are already available online, to be organized in an accessible way and provided to cartoonists as well as the rest of the community. This set of resources could provide cartoonists and other members of the community with the skills that they need to survive and thrive in the new media world.

### *The Right to Publicize*

While Rawls' theory does not specifically mandate that any individual should be given the ability to publicize justice, it seems fair to argue that society owes something to political cartoonists in this regard. Society benefits from granting this ability to cartoonists. The cartoonist sees him or herself as a government investigator, someone who can interpret society's problems and delve into rules that affect the nation. By fulfilling those roles, the cartoonist assists society in becoming more just and well-ordered. Similarly, cartoonists should be permitted to help uphold both the first and second principles of justice through publicity. The essence of the cartoonists' job allows audiences to be informed voters, such as when cartoonists point out questionable promises made by political candidates. They can highlight instances where the freedom of a particular individual or a group of people may be endangered. They also can encourage the public to utilize freedom of expression. Likewise, the cartoonist can describe situations where the least advantaged people in society are in need of assistance.

As political cartoonists have the ability to help individuals in the pursuit of justice, society owes it to cartoonists that they be allowed to serve the publicity function that is important to Rawls' well-ordered society. To support the publicity function of cartoonists, individuals need to be willing to view content that challenges their own views. They need to allow the cartoonist to guide them toward public discussions about important issues. Journalists need to be given the latitude to publish a diverse range of content, which may offend some audience members, without fear of reprisal. Cartoonists also need to be provided a platform for sharing their cartoons. That may be through a printed publication or it may be an online platform. What matters is that the cartoonist is given a place to share his or her work. By serving this publicity function, cartoonists can assist society in understanding the principles of justice as well as recognizing instances of injustice. This process should help society to arrive at a common understanding of the term justice.

Communitarians are hesitant to grant new rights to anyone. They likely would support providing cartoonists with the ability to draw cartoons that remind the community of their moral values. If cartoonists are provided the right to publicize, they must recognize that right comes with a responsibility. They have a responsibility to strengthen and support the community. Sometimes the political cartoons that gain the most attention are the ones that are the most provocative, the ones that vilify or mock members of the community. If cartoonists are going to uphold their responsibilities to the community, they must avoid those images that will disrupt or tear the community apart. They must look for ways that they can bring the community together. They should draw images that illustrate the problems in society, but they also should help the community find ways to correct those issues. They have a responsibility to ensure the health and stability of the community.

## *Freedom of Expression*

The most obvious liberty that the political cartoonist is owed through the first principle of justice is freedom of expression. The cartoonist should not have to fear for his or her life when a controversial political cartoon is published. In the eyes of Rawls, freedom of expression allows for a variety of ideas to be shared. Reasonable people are capable of seeing that variety of ideas and recognizing that they may not agree with those ideas. Rawls argues that unreasonable people:

> (1) insist as part of the public culture that their comprehensive beliefs are true; (2) want to impose their comprehensive doctrines on others; (3) reject the basic, liberal democratic political values, such as the liberal idea of persons as free and equal; and (4) do not believe that the fundamentals of the political system need to be justified to all. (Friedman 2000, 27)

Rawls suggests that unreasonable people believe that their own beliefs are the only truth. The terrorists who went to *Charlie Hebdo* and murdered 17 journalists likely fit Rawls' definition of the "unreasonable." In particular, they appear to have been convinced that their personal beliefs were the only acceptable religious doctrine. It is not unreasonable for people to have been offended by the cartoons. Individuals have the right to protest; that also is fundamental to the first principle of justice. Everyone has the right to maintain their own religious perspectives in a just society. According to Rawls, that diversity of worldviews is present in reasonable pluralism. When individuals or groups try to force people to accept a particular doctrine, they invite a divisive form of pluralism that is unhealthy for society.

The Muslim-themed cartoons that were published in *Charlie Hebdo* and other publications may be in poor taste. Indeed, *Miami Herald* cartoonist Jim Morin has said that he chooses not to draw the Prophet Muhammad in cartoons because people would focus on his decision to draw the prophet rather than the cartoon's intended message (Brown 2015). Nonetheless, Rawls would argue that the cartoonists had a right to draw and publish those cartoons. In fact, cartoonists should draw cartoons depicting Islam if they feel that the image is necessary in explaining some form of injustice in society. Similarly, the cartoonist should have the freedom to publish cartoons that depict Christianity or other religious doctrines in a poor light, particularly if the cartoonist feels as though that cartoon illustrates an infringement on justice for other people. A decision as to whether the *Charlie Hebdo* cartoons acknowledged an injustice in society goes beyond the confinements of this paper. The cartoonist, however, should be able to draw and publish those cartoons without fearing for his or her life. As explained by Graham (2007, 148), "each religion must be free to proselytize, and apostasy should be permitted, politically each religion has to accept the existence of the other."

Communitarians would not support the decision to draw cartoons that would knowingly offend one segment of the community. The right to freedom of speech should be maintained, but it should not be used in a way that damages the community. The death and devastation that has followed the publication of those cartoons clearly indicates that the cartoons did not support the health of the community. They did not illustrate a moral value. Rather, they intentionally mocked a group of people.

It is fair to argue that the freedom to publish controversial cartoons could be limited if the cartoon infringed upon the liberties of other people. Martin (1985, 53) calls this a "definitional balancing at the constitutional level." As Rawls (1996, 356) explains, speech should not be limited unless there is "no alternative way to prevent these evils than the restriction of free speech." Merely offending someone does not constitute a restriction on individual liberties.

Furthermore, the cartoonist has a responsibility to utilize the freedom of expression with care. Every right has a responsibility.

### *Freedom to Select Topics*

The second liberty that should be guaranteed to political cartoonists is freedom from physical and psychological oppression. When Rawls describes this liberty, he focuses on the concept of slavery. It is possible, however, to broaden that interpretation to look at other ways in which one might be oppressed. As Rawls (1996, 124) explains, "tyranny is unjust, exploitation is unjust." All individuals are entitled to a non-oppressive workplace. In the case of the cartoonist, a work environment might be oppressive if an editor controls the topics that cartoonist can explore in their work. If topics that might offend advertisers or audience members are prohibited, the cartoonist may feel a loss of self-respect. This might also prevent the cartoonist from being able to discuss significant issues of injustice. It is fair for editors to request that cartoonists consider particular topics for specific issues, but it is oppressive for the news organization to prevent cartoonists from selecting specific topics. Certainly the news organization retains the right to refuse publication of cartoons that could potentially infringe upon the rights of others. The cartoonist, however, should be given significant latitude in selection of topics for his or her own cartoons. If the news organization refuses to publish a particular cartoon, the organization should not prohibit the cartoonist from self-publishing that work or taking it to another news organization. Business regulations, such as non-compete clauses, that prevent an individual from publishing information at a rival news organization, would be problematic in Rawls' perspective. No regulation should infringe upon the individual liberties guaranteed by the first rule of justice. Perhaps businesses cannot be forced to publish specific content, but society owes cartoonists a flexibility in content selection. The cartoonist who chooses to publish controversial content on his or her own should not be blackballed from specific news organizations simply because he or she has published something that a particular editor did not like. Likewise, the cartoonist should not be punished for seeking an alternative venue for publishing content after a specific news organization has declined to publish it.

The communitarian would hope that the news organization would refuse to publish cartoons that might damage the community. While the cartoonist should have the right to select topics for illustration, they should select those topics with care and look for ways to support the discussion of issues rather than provoke arguments that divide the community. This may be perceived as a narrow interpretation of communitarianism. It is not intended to suggest that the community can never benefit from having an uncomfortable discussion. Sometimes cartoonists may help the community to deal with a difficult issue by encouraging discussion.

## Conclusion

Supporters of political liberalism and communitarianism view the world of the political cartoonist through different lenses. One views the cartoonist as a leader in ensuring individual liberties, while the other sees him or her as a member of the community who has a responsibility to support the needs of the collective. Like a blogger or an opinion writer, the political cartoonist can advocate for causes and also critique the state of society. The cartoonists who participated in this study generally felt that it was important for them to investigate the government, analyze complex problems, and discuss national policies. Perhaps the typical cartoon cannot provide the same degree of depth as a long, analytical news story. Nonetheless, with a few words and thoughtful imagery, political cartoonists can use artistic metaphor to deliver a poignant message that provokes discussion. Many of the survey participants felt it was important for their cartoons to interpret international news stories. The cartoonist's emphasis on the visual has the power to communicate a message that crosses language barriers. Cartoonists have the ability to remind individuals of their rights while also strengthening the community as a whole.

The participants in this survey view themselves as an extension of the fourth estate. They can analyze complex issues and succinctly articulate them, drawing connections and generalizations that may not immediately be obvious to the audience. They can remind the audience of the rights that are guaranteed to them through the first principle of justice, such as freedom of expression, the right to vote, and the freedom from psychological oppression. They can illustrate those rights in a way that is unique from the rest of the media landscape. They can highlight instances of injustice and a flawed system of resource distribution. They can publicize societal barriers that block the development of a well-ordered society. They may anger legislators, business owners, churchgoers, or anybody else in society. That anger, however, can lead to discussion, debate, and maybe even necessary change. Cartoonists should use care in provoking those discussions, however. They should emphasize the values of the community. They have a responsibility to draw cartoons that can bring the community together.

By providing political cartoonists with the skills, security, and respect that they are owed, cartoonists can continue helping society to define what justice means. Perhaps cartoonists can provoke the right discussions that will guide society to find a means to provide everyone the rights and resources that they need in order to live free, fruitful lives in a strong, cohesive community.

## DISCLOSURE STATEMENT

No potential conflict of interest was reported by the author.

## NOTES

1. The researchers compiled a list of political cartoonists from Cagle.com, Artizans.com, The Association of American Editorial Cartoonists, and the list of National and International Editorial Cartoonists available at Wikipedia.com. All 273 cartoonists were contacted via email and asked to respond to a survey online. The response rate was 34 percent.
2. The responses of the cartoonists are not exactly the same as the journalists who were asked the same series of questions in 2002, but they share some similarities. That study found that journalists felt investigating government claims, getting information out quickly, and avoiding stories with unverified information were their most important

roles. They also tended to assign a high level of importance to providing analysis and interpretation of complex problems and discussing national policy. For more information, see Weaver et al. (2007).

## REFERENCES


Ammons, David N., John C. King, and Jerry L. Yeric. 1988. "Unapproved Imagemakers: Political Cartoonists' Topic Selection, Objectivity and Perceived Restrictions." *Newspaper Research Journal* 9 (3): 79–90.

Bennett, Clay. 2016. "The Official Book." *Chattanooga Times Free Press*, April 3. http://www.timesfreepress.com/cartoons/2016/apr/03/official-book/2479/.

Borden, Sandra. 2010. "The Moral Justification for Journalism." In *Journalism Ethics: A Philosophical Approach*, edited by Christopher Meyers, 53–68. New York: Oxford University Press.

Borden, Sandra L. 2014. "Communitarian Journalism and the Common Good: Lessons from the *Catholic Worker*." *Journalism* 15 (3): 273–288.

Brown, Michael. 2015. "The Visual Art of Political Cartoons." *Visual Communication Quarterly* 22 (3): 187–190.

Christians, Clifford G., John P. Ferré, and P. Mark Fackler. 1993. *Good News: Social Ethics and the Press*. New York: Oxford University Press.

Coleman, Renita. 2000. "The Ethical Context for Public Journalism: As an Ethical Foundation for Public Journalism, Communitarian Philosophy Provides Principles for Practitioners to Apply to Real-World Problems." *Journal of Communication Inquiry* 24 (1): 41–66.

Cowell, Alan. 2006. "More European Papers Print Cartoons of Muhammad, Fueling Dispute with Muslims." *The New York Times*, February 2. http://www.nytimes.com/2006/02/02/international/europe/02danish.html?pagewanted=all&_r=0.

Culbertson, Hugh M., and Ni Chen. 1997. "Communitarianism: A Foundation for Communication Symmetry." *Public Relations Quarterly* 42 (2): 36–41.

Darkow, John. 2011. "Poverty in America." *Columbia Daily Tribune*, September 16. http://www.nytimes.com/2011/09/14/us/14census.html.

Etzioni, Amitai. 1993. *The Sprit of Commuinity: Rights, Responsibilities, and The Communitarian Agenda*. New York: Crown Publishers.

Friedman, Marilyn. 2000. "John Rawls and the Political Coercion of Unreasonable People." In *The Idea of a Political Liberalism*, edited by Victoria Davion and Clark Wolf, 16–33. Oxford: Rowman & Littlefield.

Graham, Paul. 2007. *Rawls*. Oxford: Oneworld Publications.

Guyer, Jonathan. 2015. "The Offending Art: Political Cartooning after the Charlie Hebdo Attacks." *Neiman Reports*, March 24. http://niemanreports.org/articles/the-offending-art-political-cartooning-after-the-charlie-hebdo-attacks/.

Harrison, Randall P. 1981. *The Cartoon: Communication to the Quick*. Beverly Hills, CA: Sage.

Herb Block Foundation. 2011. "The Golden Age for Editorial Cartoonists at the Nation's Newspapers is Over." http://www.herbblockfoundation.org/sites/default/files/imce_uploads/pdfs/hbf2011whitepaper_f1.pdf.

Higgins, Andrews, and Dan Bilefsky. 2015. "French Police Storm Hostage Sites, Killing Gunmen." *The New York Times*, January 9. http://www.nytimes.com/2015/01/10/world/europe/charlie-hebdo-paris-shooting.html.

Kaplan, Sarah. 2016. "Mississippi's Senate Just Approved a Sweeping "Religious Liberty" Bill that Critics Say is the Worst yet for LGBT Rights." *The Washington Post*, March 31. https://www.washingtonpost.com/news/morning-mix/wp/2016/03/31/mississippis-senate-just-approved-a-sweeping-religious-liberty-bill-that-critics-say-is-the-worst-yet-for-lgbt-rights/?tid=a_inl.

Maffettone, Sebastiano. 2010. *Rawls: An Introduction*. Malden, MA: Polity Press.

Martin, Rex. 1985. *Rawls and Rights*. Lawrence, KA: University of Kansas Press.

Müller, Marion G., Esra Özcan, and Ognyan Scizov. 2009. "Dangerous Depictions: A Visual Case Study of Contemporary Cartoon Controversies." *Popular Communication* 7: 28–39.

Neuberger, Lindsay, and Marina Kremar. 2008. "Exploring the Effects of Editorial Cartoons on Attitude Change: An Experimental Analysis." Paper Presented at the Annual Meeting of the International Communication Association, Montreal, Canada.

Rawls, John. 1991. *A Theory of Justice*. Oxford: Oxford University Press.

Rawls, John. 1996. *Political Liberalism*. New York: Columbia University Press.

Riffe, Daniel, Donald Sneed, and Roger L. Van Ommeren. 1985. "Behind the Editorial Page Cartoon." *Journalism Quarterly* 62 (2): 378–450.

Rogers, Rob. 2014. "Known Soldier." *Pittsburgh Post-Gazette*, November 13. http://blogs.post-gazette.com/opinion/rob-rogers-cartoons/42890-known-soldier.

Tanner, Kristi. 2016. "All Flint's Children must be Treated as Exposed to Lead." *The Detroit Free Press*, Janurary 16. http://www.freep.com/story/opinion/contributors/raw-data/2016/01/16/map-8657-flints-youngest-children-exposed-lead/78818888/.

Tavernise, Sabrina. 2011. "Soaring Poverty Casts Spotlight on 'Lost Decade'." *The New York Times*, September 13. http://www.nytimes.com/2011/09/14/us/14census.html.

Telnaes, Ann. 2015. "A Cartoon Defying the Paris Terrorists." *The Washington Post*, January 7. https://www.washingtonpost.com/news/opinions/wp/2015/01/07/at-least-12-killed-at-french-satirical-magazine/.

Telnaes, Ann. 2016. "Mississippi's 'Religious Liberty' Bill is Pure Discrimination." *The Washington Post*, April 4. https://www.washingtonpost.com/news/opinions/wp/2016/04/04/mississippis-religious-liberty-bill-is-pure-discrimination/.

Thompson, Mike. 2015. "Where did $6 Billion of Your Tax Money Go?" *Detroit Free Press*, March 10. http://www.freep.com/story/opinion/columnists/mike-thompson/2016/03/10/flint-lead-isis/81581524/.

Varvel, Gary. 2015. "Cartoonist Gary Varvel: Terrorists Attack Paris Newspaper. *Indianapolis Star*, Janurary 7. http://www.indystar.com/story/opinion/cartoons/2015/01/07/cartoonist-gary-varvel-terrorists-attack-paris-newspaper/21386127/.

Weaver, David, Randal A. Beam, Bonnie J. Brownlee, Paul S. Voakes, and G. Cleveland Wilhoit. 2007. *The American Journalist in the 21st Century*. Mahwah, NJ: Lawrence Erlbaum Associates.

Zyglis, Adam. 2016. "N.C. Bathroom Bill." *Buffalo News*, April 2. http://adamzyglis.buffalonews.com/2016/04/02/nc-bathroom-bill/.

# THE NETWORKS OF GLOBAL JOURNALISM
## Global news construction through the collaboration of global news startups with freelancers

**Lea Hellmueller, Sadia Ehsan Cheema,** and **Xu Zhang**

*This study explores how recent global news startups have connected freelancers with traditional news organizations. Through 10 interviews with founders and editors, the results reveal a networked marketplace of global journalism: the startups build on new technologies as well as on-the-ground evidence as their business model and de-localize the distribution of news within a digital marketplace. Supplemented by a content analysis of their edited stories (N = 226), global journalism as an outcome of this marketplace is discussed.*

### Introduction

Mounting threats to foreign correspondents are putting international news coverage at risk, as exemplified by the murders of James Foley and Steven Sotloff in Syria in 2014. Foley and Sotloff, both freelance journalists at the time (Mahoney 2015), personify the increasing numbers of freelance journalists in war regions who place their lives at risk to conduct global news coverage (Bender 2014). On one hand, the status quo is that legacy news organizations are closing their bureaus overseas. In the United States, for example, the number of traditional full-time newspaper foreign correspondents dropped from 307 in 2003 to 234 in 2011—a decline of about 25 percent—whereas television network coverage of global news was less than half in 2013 compared to the late 1980s (Pew Research Center 2014). On the other hand, despite legacy news organizations closing their bureaus overseas, the numbers of foreign freelancers have increased (Dyer 2014). Safety issues have become particularly concerning, as according to the Committee to Protect Journalists, journalists were killed at a high rate in 2014, with the Middle East being the most dangerous region to work for journalists (Committee to Protect Journalists 2014). The organization argues that at least 60 journalists were killed globally in 2014 compared with 70 who died in 2013. In particular, freelance journalists face many challenges: they often write for multiple outlets, do not have the same types of safety protection and insurance that traditional foreign correspondents have, and receive lower pay than salaried reporters (Bender 2014). In response to the increasing challenges that freelance journalists face, global news startups have emerged to organize freelance journalism labor and to collaborate with freelancers to sell their work to legacy news organizations.

Within the past 10 years, global news startups have been launched in different parts of the world, such as Russia, Germany, France, the United Kingdom, and the United States

(Dyer 2014). Such startups act as intermediaries between traditional news organizations and freelance journalists. In most cases, freelancers and publishers can sign up on websites of startups to participate in the exchange of news story pitches and final products such as photographs or video coverage of a specific event. News organizations are encouraged to assign the coverage and ask for pitches.[1] Once a story is decided on, a news organization can work directly with reporters to share requirements specific to the outlet, such as the case in ARA Network. Startups reflect a transition toward a "global news arena," which Reese (2008, 241) defines as the "reach, interconnectedness and virtually real-time properties of a globalized media that contribute to our experiencing the world as a whole, shaping the intensity and nature of that experience."

The present study seeks to explore the *interconnectedness* (Reese 2010) between global news startups and freelance journalists. In the efforts of freelance journalists to provide information to multiple audiences across the world, what protections and support should freelancers be able to count on during a time when journalists around the world have been shot, beheaded, and quarantined? How does the network of startups connect freelancers with traditional news organizations, and how does the digital network affect the construction of global journalism? Through interviews with founders and editors of 10 global news startups, this study conceptualizes the network flow of foreign news and the global discourse that is presented by stories produced or initiated by global news startups. Furthermore, it is proposed that these online global freelance ventures provide a starting point for scholars to identify the key practices and normative ideas that define global journalism's story-telling culture in the digital age.

## Global Journalism and News Spaces

Global journalism serves as the theoretical foundation of this study (Reese 2015; Waisbord and Mellado 2014). Indeed, globalization has posed many challenges for journalism—one of them being the categorization of news as either domestic or foreign. Berglez (2008, 845) explained that "Global journalism transgresses and transcends the traditional domestic–foreign dichotomy" and should be analyzed in terms of news production and news consumption from a global perspective. Although nation-state boundaries previously permitted domestic news production and consumption, the boundaries have recently become blurred: Beck (2005) and Sassen (1996) stated that nation-states are being more or less controlled by external global powers such as global economics and capital, international relations, and foreign policies. The ideology posed by the nation-state can also be seen as operating under the realm of "national outlook" (Beck 2005, 111) with the focus of news framing on nation-states, whereas a broader term of "global outlook" can be attributed to these external global powers that seek to "understand and explain how economic, political, social and ecological practices, processes and problems in different parts of the world affect each other, are interlocked, or share commonalities" (Berglez 2008, 847).

With the rise of global connectivity, the conceptual boundaries of journalism have shifted and new forms are emerging (as in the case with the global news startups), which all point to a network space in which journalism is performed: "This extends to the broader deliberative arena to which journalism contributes, a space now often loosely deemed a networked public sphere, or even a global networked sphere" (Reese 2016, 3). For many years, journalists have been studied under the umbrella of news organizations. Level of hierarchy and gatekeeping theory (Shoemaker and Reese 2014; Shoemaker and Vos 2009) proposes individual journalists to be embedded within an organizational level of influence over their work and professional attitudes. Following this idea, journalistic culture is conceptualized as being shaped by the economic, political, and legal system in which journalists operate (Shoemaker and Reese 2014).

Meanwhile, Reese (2016) suggested that the new networked spaces make the concepts of *fields*, *spheres*, and *networks* much more relevant and require thinking beyond institutional terms of news organizations as previously conceptualized in the level-of-influence models. Freelance journalists have become important in covering foreign events. On the other hand, freelancers have been understudied because their employment status is not linked to a news organization and they increasingly work across media platforms (Palmer 2015); hence, they are rarely polled in surveys of journalists and not much is known about how they work (Hanitzsch and Wahl-Jorgensen 2009). Different configurations of global journalism (Reese 2016) have made networks outside of the organizational structure much more relevant than in the pre-digital age. The case of freelance journalists is just one among many: the blurring links between professional journalists, marketing professionals, and various corporations provide a new way of thinking about journalism (Reese 2016). In terms of global journalism, the network space has no unique geographical location. Those news-networked spaces that have no geographical location introduce new methodological challenges: the social actors and their practices have to be identified. Meanwhile, Lewis and Usher (2013) explained that the connection of journalists to other fields—like technology—opens journalism up to greater transparency about the construction of news. Hence, the examination of global news startups can enrich scholarly knowledge regarding the practices of global digital news networks as well as the form of global journalism produced by the network of global news startups.

## *Global News Startups*

Global news startups—both for-profit and non-profit—are defined by their main mission of connecting buyers and sellers in the world of foreign news (Dyer 2014). Their funding mechanisms are as diverse as the startups themselves (see Table 1): self-sustaining non-profit, self-sustaining for-profit, self-sustaining, ventures, and funding depending on independent investors. Funding that is not tied to bank loans or debit structures isolates new companies from short-term profit so they can instead focus on innovation, experimentation, and growth (Carlson and Usher 2015; Ries 2011). Carlson and Usher (2015, 3) pointed out that one major criterion of news startups is their need to explain their unique contribution to an existing industry, to differentiate their products from other startup organizations.

Within the diversity of funding mechanisms, it is essential to understand how global news startups initiate collaboration with freelancers. In this study, the foreign news startups are conceptualized as the centers of the network (see Figure 1), because they are the ones initiating the construction of foreign news in a digital news environment. Startups are connected to buyers, news organizations, freelancers, marketers, and content managers; their connectional ties build a network of collaboration. The way startups communicate and exchange services and products within their networks marks their identity and creates a new (diverse) digital marketplace to produce global news.

**TABLE 1**
Global news startups selected for this study

| Foreign news startup | Year founded (location) | Number of employees | Major clients | Niche market |
|---|---|---|---|---|
| ARA Network | 2008 (Berlin, Germany) | 8 | *USA Today*, *Washington Times* | Works like a co-op. Edits stories |
| GRN Live | 2000 (London, UK) | 5 | Australian Broadcasting Corporation | For-profit. Works mostly with radio and broadcasters |
| NewsFixed | 2014 (London, UK) | 6 | Al Jazeera, *The Economist* | Connects editors with journalists |
| Newsmodo | 2013 (Melbourne, Australia) | 8 | *The Sun*, NBC | Branded content combined with journalistic content |
| Storyful | 2010 (Dublin, Ireland) | 100 | *The Wall Street Journal*, *The New York Times* | Bought by News Corp in 2013 for $25 million. Acquires and verifies freelancers' and citizen journalists' videos for news outlets and obtains licenses for videos found on social media |
| Storyhunter | 2012 (Brooklyn, NY, USA) | 10 | Fusion | Primarily videographers, connects journalists like a dating site |
| Worldcrunch | 2011 (Paris, France) | 10 | *New York Times* syndicate | Obtains licenses to translate and sell stories from major newspapers to English-language publications |
| Hack Pack | 2014 (Moscow, Russia) | 6 | | Connects journalists in Russia and other parts of the world with media organizations worldwide |

Source: Adapted from Dyer (2014).

### *Freelance Journalists' Role in the News Network*

The emergence of global news startups offers a constitutive moment to examine the changing roles of freelancers within the network of global journalism (see Figure 1). Television news outlets are relying more than ever on freelance employees because foreign news coverage depends on the eyewitness accounts of journalists on the ground (Paterson and Sreberny 2004). Freelance journalists are broadly defined as "self-employed journalists in the media industries who deliver material to the press, electronic media, the Internet, and information businesses" (Edström and Ladendorf 2012, 711). Several scholars have recently noted a greater reliance of media organizations on freelancers or outsourced labor (Palmer 2015) and the fact that freelancing is growing more rapidly than ever in all industries and not just in the news business (Prosser 2015). Prosser (2015) wrote, "Entrepreneurial workers in Britain and the US are turning to self-employment in such large numbers that half the working population in both countries could be their own boss within five years." In the

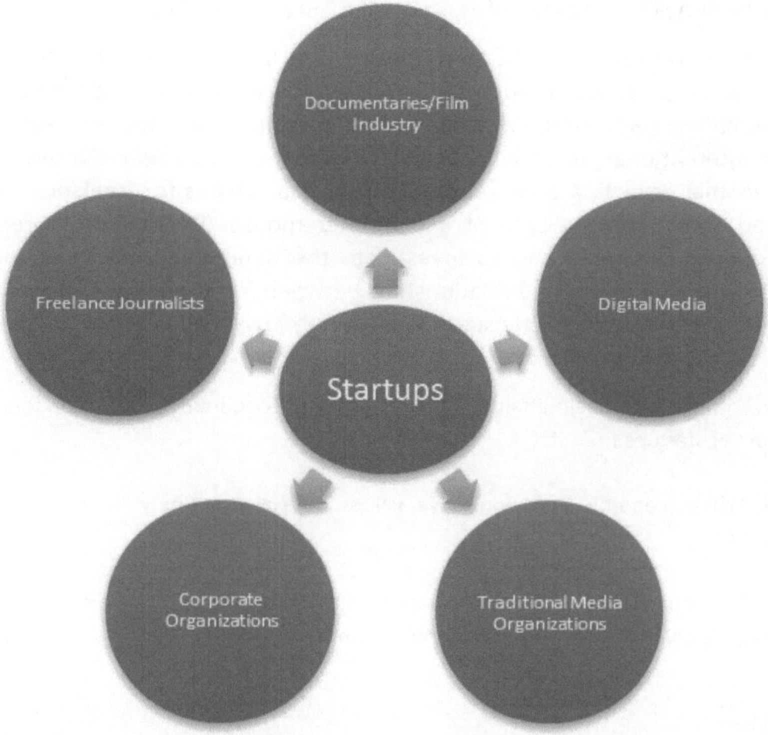


**FIGURE 1**
The network of global news startups

news business, this shift has been intensified by new technologies that deeply affect journalistic work. Ryan (2009), as well as Paterson and Sreberny (2004), discussed the economic shifts of media businesses that have led to the closure of foreign bureaus and the ways in which television news outlets are increasingly relying on freelance employees to receive footage and eyewitness accounts from on the ground.

Freelance journalists often work across various media but also across professions: nearly half of the freelance journalists in Germany, for example, also do public relations work (Meyen and Springer 2009). Thus, freelancers work across a gap between journalism and public relations. Those different normative approaches may put freelance journalists into difficult situations (Barth and Donsbach 1992), as they sometimes have to navigate conflicting roles.

Meanwhile, global news startups contribute to a potential conflict of normative roles because startups employ freelancers from around the world to not only cover international news but also produce branded content (Dyer 2014, 35). From a news perspective, the repercussions of such practices are enormous when US media such as *The New York Times*, *The Washington Post*, *The Wall Street Journal*, Fox News, and others buy stories and engage freelancers that are registered with those startups. Hence, the first research question assesses the impact of increased collaboration between freelancers and startups and the quality of those relationships:

> **RQ1:** What types of collaborations do startups initiate with freelance journalists?

Freelance journalists' working conditions are understudied, and the collaboration with startups is an important new research inquiry in understanding how global journalism—as exemplified in this emerging collaboration—shapes the success of international storytelling. Do these global startups seek out, edit, and sell global news that reflects a global outlook? The main idea is for freelance journalists to be hired with a simple click of a computer mouse (Dyer 2014). Three further research questions were posed to investigate the defining elements of the global digital journalistic networks and relationships between freelancers and global startups, and the extent stories pitched by startups or covered by freelance journalists embrace elements of global journalism:

> **RQ2:** With what global journalistic roles, values, and economic principles do founders and editors of startups identify?
>
> **RQ3:** What economic and normative values do startups apply to their collaborative network?
>
> **RQ4:** To what extent do freelance stories or stories pitched by startups cover global spaces, global identities, and global powers in news stories?

## Method

Based on initial readings, this study conceptualizes *global news startups* as initiators of global news networks (see Figure 1). Thus, the investigation began by interviewing the founders of the most established and well-known global news startup organizations. The interviews were conducted with six male and four female editors/founders of eight global news startups. Most of the interviewees were previously employed journalists and foreign correspondents at news media outlets in the United States, Australia, the United Kingdom, Germany, Italy, France, and Russia, with an average experience of 15 years for each person in journalism and news production.

The global news startups in this study (see Table 1) were selected based on their international orientation, their connections to foreign freelance journalists, and their spotlight during their launch in industry blogs of the Nieman Journalism Lab and *Nieman Reports*. Thus, the sample presented in this study is global news startups that have gained scholarly and industry attention in recent years. This criterion results in excluding startups that produce stories in languages other than English. The global dominance of the English language not only sets a limitation on this study's sampling strategy but also a limitation in the production and diversity of international news (as often mentioned in interviews with founders of those startups). Most of the global news startups interviewed in this study wish to engage more non-English-language freelancers to produce stories in other languages but at the same time must cater to an audience that consumes digital news in English. The limitation of this type of global journalism is discussed in the analysis section.

This study examines the work and practices of eight major global news startup ventures. A mixed-methods approach was used to address the research questions, because a more holistic view can be gained by combining different methods in one research study

(Tashakkori and Teddlie 2003). Mixed-methods designs are defined as "the use of two (or more) research methods in a single study, when one (or more) of the methods is not complete in itself" (Morse and Niehaus 2009, 9).

The research began with a qualitative search for the meanings that the founders of global startups assigned to their global journalism networks. Launching from this qualitative inquiry on global journalism, a content analysis was conducted on the practices and stories produced by those startups.

### *Qualitative Interviews*

The study of global news startup practices requires intensive understanding of their organizations' functionalities, philosophies, and journalism ethics and practices. These data were collected through in-depth interviews of founders and editors of the global ventures listed in the previous section. Interviews are useful to analyze content by connecting text to human actors, and they serve as tools for understanding how startup founders view the nature of their work (Deuze 2005). Interviewing freelance journalists or founders of startups poses challenges, as the journalistic profession has expanded and become more complex due to digitalization. In this new era, the major challenge is to convince journalists (as well as founders of startups) to allocate time for an interview (Lewis and Reese 2009).

For this study, 10 interviews were conducted with founders and editors of eight global news startups: ARA Network, GRN Live, NewsFixed, Newsmodo, Storyful, Storyhunter, Worldcrunch, and Hack Pack (see Table 1). Of those interviewed, eight were conducted with founders of the startups and two with editors of the startup organizations. All of the interviewed founders and editors had a background in foreign reporting. The startups were contacted via email starting in September 2015, and these founders and editors agreed to be interviewed. The interviews were conducted between the end of November and the beginning of March via Skype because the founders and editors worked across Eastern and Western Europe, Australia, and North America. The interviews ranged from 40 to 90 minutes, with an average time of about 55 minutes. The participants were asked to talk about their founding strategies, provide their organizations' philosophies and business model, ethics and practices when interacting with freelancers and buyers, and their perception of how their service provides better work opportunities for freelance journalists. The main idea was to understand the digital global network that is defining the business and journalistic practices of those newly emerged startup organizations. After the collection of the interview data, the interviews were transcribed and then textually analyzed with the qualitative analysis program Ethnograph 6.0.

### *Content Analysis*

For answering the last research question, a quantitative content analysis examined how the three main building blocks of global journalism—space, identity, and power—were reflected in news stories pitched by freelancers or startups to address whether stories produced by the freelancers included a global perspective. Riffe, Lacy, and Fico (2014, 19) described quantitative content analysis as a "systematic, replicable and statistical method in which to describe the communication, draw inferences about its meaning or infer from the communication to its context." In this study, the unit of analysis is each single textual news item published on the websites of ARA Network and Worldcrunch.

### *Sampling*

Among the startups in our sample, ARA Network and Worldcrunch were the only two that edited the stories submitted by the freelancers. The other startups did not edit the stories, so the stories of ARA Network and Worldcrunch were investigated to understand how international stories are covered by global news startups. Both organizations have online news archives on their websites. For selecting news stories from ARA Network and Worldcrunch, the study established the time frame of news publications from November 1, 2015, to February 29, 2016, which also matches the time frame of the interview with startup personnel. A stratified sampling (by month) of five randomly selected weekdays per week was drawn, which resulted in a total sample of 80 days. From this, 85 news stories were selected from ARA Network and 141 news stories were selected from Worldcrunch. A total of 226 news stories were analyzed.

### *Coding Scheme*

The creation of a coding scheme was based on the notion of global journalism. Each variable measured the power, space, and identity accordingly. By measuring these variables, the study was able to examine what kinds of news discourse were actually produced by the freelancers. Seven variables were coded: media organization served by the startup, journalists' employment status, news story type, news topics, main source, main source's identity, and news discourse.

First, the geographical region of the news organization that published the story was coded. It included the following categories: North America, Central America, South America, Western Europe, Eastern Europe, Africa, Eastern Asia, Southern Asia, Western Asia, and Oceania (Australia and New Zealand).

The variable "journalists' employment status" included domestic journalist, foreign correspondent, freelancer, and expert. The categories were coded as mutually exclusive to understand whether the reporter was a staff reporter of an organization or a freelance journalist paid by the organization per story. In most cases, employment status was determined by the reporter's Twitter biography that declared his or her affiliation. The variable "news story type" included four categories: brief, article, feature/chronicle, and opinion piece. The variable "news topics" consisted of what news topics were covered by the startups. This included a wide range of categories, such as election/campaign, government/legislature, geopolitics, police and crime, terrorism, courts, defense/military, economy, education, energy/climate change/environment, accidents/natural disasters, health, religion, immigration, human rights, demonstrations, social problems, housing, and transportation. The variable "main source" measured the primary news source on which the selected news item relied or from which the story originated. This variable had 10 categories: government, business, military, expert (not part of the other categories), media outlet, international organization, ordinary people, civil society, and anonymous. Also, the variable "news source identity" measured the geographical identity of the primary news sources to see what voices are covered in a local community. This variable included different geographical regions, such as North America, Central America, Western Europe, Eastern Asia, and so forth.

Last, the variable "news discourse" measured how a news story was covered in terms of geographical space. It included several categories, such as local event/local discourse, which meant the news story covers the impact of a local event on local people. Another example was transnational event/global discourse, which measured the impact of global events on different parts of the world.

Two trained coders each coded the same 10 percent of the entire sample to test inter-coder reliability. A total of 22 news stories from 226 were randomly selected to check for levels of agreement between two independent coders working on 19 different variables. The coding focused on the textual content of the selected news items. The inter-coder reliability determined by Krippendorff's alpha was 1 for client served, 0.72 for journalist employment, 0.92 for story type, 0.85 for news story topic, from 0.81 to 1 for each source variable, 0.84 for main source, 0.88 for main source identity, and 0.89 for news discourse. Aside from Krippendorff's alpha, the study also checked the *p* percentage agreement. All coded variables achieved greater than 81 percent agreement. The final results of inter-coder reliability were acceptable.

## Findings: Textual Analysis

This section discusses the themes that emerged from the qualitative interviews. In total, eight overarching themes were found. The immediate experience of founders and editors with the news industry informs their business rationales: in most cases, the motivation to build a network between traditional news organization and freelancers came about because of experience in the field. The most frequent reason cited by the startup personnel was concern over a lack of professional news resources to cover foreign events. Another motive was to start something that would be of value to a global audience and to take advantage of the knowledge on the ground held by freelancers around the world. Startup personnel agreed that foreign freelancers are crucial in a more interconnected world and that the current system does not optimize the knowledge and resources that freelancers offer. Meanwhile, they believed there is a lack of consistent practices (i.e., isomorphism) among startup ideologies and business strategies. The variety of ideas and social purposes of startups as outlined by the founders were overlapping and sometimes even conflicting based on mainly a liberal market ideal: the decline in audience attention; the shift to digital news; the decline in revenue that leads to the consideration of new, innovative ways to connect resources that are available (i.e., audience interests, freelance labor, the need for international stories); and to build a network of those resources to produce on-the-ground international reporting for an emerging, globally connected audience. Overall, the motivations are ideologically as well as financially motivated to build a startup for foreign news. What is interesting, however, are the blurring lines to other fields. Startups that do not edit stories and are for-profit take on more branded content that is produced by freelance journalists; this provides an important income for both startups and freelance journalists. Some startup founders held the mirror toward the news industry itself:

> You know, and I think this is the general sentiment in the public and the journalism world … if people think the major news organizations in the world are not dictated by economic interests, then you know, I think they are dreaming, because all news organizations are run by someone with a particular interest, so I think, of course, brands have to be much more open and honest. And yes, they are dictated by economic interest, but I think it is the same in the journalism world. (Founder A)

Another formative element for startups was that the interviewees seemed to connect new technologies to their nature of work, which enabled them to reach out to global clients, freelancers, and audiences that build their business network. The use of technology was seen as a prerequisite for innovation and was seen to influence the startups' daily operations, networking, and journalistic practices.

Table 2 provides the major themes identified and shared by all the startups. The themes identified in this textual analysis were shared by startups that edit stories and those that do not. The textual analysis of the interviews was paired with content analysis of the news stories of global startups that edit the stories. Table 2 provides an overview of the themes shared by both categories of startups (i.e., editing and non-editing global startups).

### *Global Clients*

All the startups were international in their clientele reach. The startups served media throughout the world and sold stories to many local broadcast and print media services in various regions. The clients from the United States included *The Washington Post*, *The Wall Street Journal*, *The New York Times*, ABC News, and Fox News, among others.

Many of the startup founders and editors mentioned that the majority of their clients are in the United States and reflect the dominance of the English language within the paradigm of global news. One of the founders of a startup said,

> The majority of our clients are in the US ... but we do sell to Germany; we sell to Switzerland, Denmark; and Canada is a regular client. We have worked for the British, Irish, Australian ... so you know we worked all over. We just never had the time or the capacity to resell in a lot of languages. (Founder B)

In terms of language selection, nearly all of the founders and editors mentioned that the English language is dominant in global journalism. One startup founder said, "Most of the stories are in English and the reason being is providing services to international audiences" (Founder D).

**TABLE 2**
Main themes identified through source quotes in qualitative interviews

| | | Theme found in interviews | |
|---|---|---|---|
| **Theme** | **Definition of theme** | *N* | % |
| Global clients | Clients served, global reach | 13 | 6.34 |
| Globalization and news discourse | Client expectations, audience expectations, types of stories and news discourse | 47 | 22.93 |
| Unique business model, freelancer practices, and journalism ethics | Digital footprint to freelancers, conduit between freelancers and clients, verification procedures to sustain journalistic reporting ethics | 112 | 54.63 |
| Benefits to freelancers | Increased job opportunities, secured payments, provide promotional and reputational support, and other support mechanisms (editing, training, correspondence with clients, etc.) | 33 | 16.09 |

*N* = 205 (total number of codes).

Another founder mentioned that the startup tries to be global in reach by covering news in all areas, except "dark zones" or crisis areas:

> We really do try to keep it global ... um, even though our staff is largely—you know—based in the US, and Europe, and Australia; the stories are coming from everywhere. So we do a lot of Middle Eastern coverage, and we are covering Europe and the US, and Australia a lot just because there is a lot of social news that comes out of those areas, but if there is something that is social, we are going to try and cover it wherever it is. It does lead to some natural dark zones, you know. China is a difficult place to work within because of the firewalls there. (Founder E)

### *Globalization and News Discourse*

Globalization seemed to play a major role in the operation of these startups. Nearly all startups stated that globalization has influenced the demand of international news, in terms of both audience expectations and client expectations. In terms of audience expectations, globalization has spiked interest among readers wanting to know more about other places, perhaps because of how the international market has changed the knowledge of audiences, such as through multinational corporations and entertainment industries operating in different regions. One of the founders said, "You know, there is something called a 'global story' to which most of the world is paying attention" (Founder D).

In terms of client expectations, globalization has affected the way journalism operates at large. News clients with limited resources can now tell stories from places they do not have a staff on the ground. One editor mentioned,

> Globalization makes it very easy for us to cover news in the same way it would be covered locally but would hurt the capabilities of our clients to do themselves. So that's where they come to us and that is where our experiences of global content comes in. (Editor D)

The impact of globalization on audience and client expectations tends to direct the news topics and discourses of these startups. Most of these startups overlapped on various news topics they covered for the clients and seemed to cluster around global discourses. Nearly all of the interviewees mentioned that they covered news centered on human rights, terrorism, politics, immigration, education, cultural and global heritage, international or local criminal activities, global warming, health, energy and environment, elections, crises, and entertainment. Nearly all of these topics centered on transnational and global discourses, which indicates that these startups engage in news reporting that affects international audiences at large. One of the editors of the startup said,

> We want to create a news product that is global in nature and has a mix of point of views and wide range of coverage of stories from all across the world so that our potential subscribers know that we provide them with a unique opportunity to get a global perspective of the world. (Editor A)

### *Unique Business Model, Freelancer Practices, and Journalism Ethics*

These global startups use a business model that provides a bridge between freelancers and clients. Nearly all founders and editors of the startups mentioned that their premise is to provide a digital footprint to freelancers, provide them with an avenue to build their own profile, and connect them with media outlets such as magazines and newspapers, and help the clients expand their news-reporting capabilities to capture content and cover stories around the world. These startups usually have an editorial team and a network of journalists all around the world to sell stories to global clients. They connect freelancers to traditional news organizations (or whoever wants to buy a journalistic product), and they mediate the relationship by overseeing the correspondence between clients and journalists and ensuring that journalists provide quality work to the clients. One of the editors said,

> So we just manage … we do a lot of work to make sure that when a freelancer comes and asks for an idea, you know, we have to edit it and make sure it's really interesting and that it's well written and that it has everything that it needs, so that it will be chosen. Because, you know, a lot of the time, that's how we are supporting the freelancers … quite often, things will come in that, you know will be lazily written, so we fix it up and we make it near the top quality, and we say to the publisher, "Oh, look at this fantastic story!" (Editor B)

The most important aspect of their business model is to ensure that they sell premium products to their clients to sustain businesses. Therefore, the startups engage in verification processes at two levels. The first level is verifying the journalists' qualifications and experience in the field. Having a comprehensive online sign-up process for journalists and checking references to verify their credibility achieves this. The second level of the verification process is to ensure that the freelancer has followed ethical practices in reporting the stories. One of the editors mentioned,

> This is one of the biggest challenges in the industry. Every situation is different, so there is no magic-bullet answer to how different scenarios verify. There is a lot of ways that you can verify different ideas, elements of stories and a lot of that goes down to ideas getting second opinions or second- or third-party inputs to verify things that have happened. We often will request details of any interviewees and verify if there was any reason to have any concern or involvement in stories. We also provide the journalists' details to the clients as well. (Editor D)

The diverse and unique business models of startups are not only set up in a way that the business serves as a conduit between freelancers and clients but also includes contractual agreements, verification processes, and procedures at all levels to ensure that quality news stories are sold to clients.

### *Benefits for Freelancers*

Founders and editors of global news startups mentioned that their business model provides more job opportunities for freelancers across the world in the form of secured pay for freelancers so they utilize their reporting skills and are able to make a living off their work. It also reduces the burden from freelancers in terms of communication with clients, as the startup engages in that process. This allows freelancers to focus on building their work profile and achieve credibility over time. The business model of these global startups also provides freelancers with some unique platforms for their work to be published. One of the editors mentioned,

> I mean, we do all of the administrative stuff. We do all of the editing ... we do, you know ... we do all of the client communication so that they do not have to do any of that. They just sit at home with the story, which is kind of good. We also promote them, so that we have a page on our website of efficient freelancers, and we promote the people we work with the most often, that are working hard and that are doing the best jobs. So we try to always support the people that are working closely with us. And yeah, in the same regard, we recommend people that are of high value and that have worked with us a lot and that we know we will continue to recommend them when more work comes in, so, basically we support them if they support us, I suppose. (Editor E)

These online platforms not only provide promotional and reputational support to freelancers but also a structure for them to engage with their community online. The founder of one of the startups mentioned:

> The online platform provides a structure for freelance journalists that they don't get elsewhere. Moreover, it's a community to a degree. So it's like in the old days when you had newsroom meetings. In time, we will provide that functionality and allow freelancers to communicate between themselves about the industry and the issues. (Founder C)

Another major benefit to freelancers is that these startups engage in practices that informally train them on skills required to be a successful freelancer. They train them on sharpening their story pitches, the practices of writing stories, ethical practices in journalism, and the practicalities of being a freelancer. All of these benefits highlight how freelancers can grow their profiles by providing services to these startups and, in addition, refine their journalistic practices and skills to better serve the media client.

## Clients Served by Startups: Results from the Content Analysis

The last research question asked to what extent freelance stories or stories pitched by startups cover global spaces, identities, and global powers (Berglez 2008). Because the interviews allude to the purpose of global storytelling in journalism initiated by the foreign startups, the following content analysis evaluates—based on the theoretical framework of global journalism—how the stories are edited and published. Furthermore, the differences and similarities are of interest to understand the heterogeneities among global news startups. For answering the research question, this study first measured the geographical location of media clients served by the two startups of ARA Network (headquartered in Germany) and Worldcrunch (headquartered in France). The statistical analysis pointed to a significant difference between ARA Network and Worldcrunch in terms of geographical location of their media clients, $\chi^2(8) = 164.741$, $p < 0.001$. For ARA Network, among the total number of articles, 82 of them were from North America (96.5 percent) and 2 of them were from Western Asia[2] (2.4 percent). By contrast, in 141 articles by Worldcrunch, 14 (9.9 percent) were from North American media outlets, 3 (2.1 percent) were from Central American media, and 15 (10.6 percent) represented South American media. The majority of those articles were published by Western European media outlets (79, 56 percent) and another 3 (2.1 percent) were from Eastern European media. African (7, 5 percent), Western Asian (5, 3.5 percent), and Eastern Asian (6, 4.3 percent) media outlets were also represented (see Table 3).

### *Journalists' Employment Status*

This study measured the authorship of news articles published on the websites of two startups. The retrieved test statistics indicated that there is a significant difference between ARA Network and Worldcrunch in terms of the news writers' employment status, $\chi^2(4) = 82.69$, $p < 0.001$. For ARA Network, published news articles were mostly written by freelance journalists (63, 74.1 percent). In contrast, a majority of Worldcrunch stories were written by domestic journalists (79, 56 percent) and 22 news stories were written by freelancers (15.6 percent). In other words, startups can also connect domestic and full-time journalists and provide those with additional work and opportunities to have their work published.

### *News Story Type and Topics*

For both startups, the article is the most common story type (ARA Network, 68, 80 percent; Worldcrunch, 73, 51.8 percent). For Worldcrunch, there were also 24 (17 percent) feature stories. News articles retrieved from ARA Network and Worldcrunch covered a wide range of news topics. The test statistics showed a significant difference between ARA Network and Worldcrunch in terms of news topics covered, $\chi^2(17) = 52.61$, $p < 0.001$. For ARA Network, terrorism was the most widely covered topic (21, 24.7 percent). Another widely covered topic was related to energy, environment, and climate change (11, 12.9 percent). For Worldcrunch, the most frequently covered topic was geopolitics (32, 22.7 percent). Similar to ARA Network, terrorism (24, 17 percent) was also extensively covered by Worldcrunch.

### *Main Source Identity*

This variable connected with another building block of global journalism: identity. The retrieved test statistics indicated that the two startups relied on different regional news actors to cover the news stories, $\chi^2(10) = 20.25$, $p = 0.027$. Specifically, for both startups, sources from Western Europe were mostly featured in news articles (ARA Network, 34, 40 percent; Worldcrunch, 43, 30.5 percent). On the other hand, Worldcrunch included more sources from Western Asia (30, 21.3 percent) and North America (26, 18.4 percent) (Table 5).

**TABLE 3**
Geographical location of clients served by startups

| | ARA Network | | Worldcrunch | |
|---|---|---|---|---|
| **Geographical location** | *N* | % | *N* | % |
| North America | 82 | 96.5 | 14 | 9.9 |
| Central America | 0 | 0 | 3 | 2.1 |
| South America | 0 | 0 | 15 | 10.6 |
| Western Europe | 1 | 1.2 | 79 | 56 |
| Eastern Europe | 0 | 0 | 3 | 2.1 |
| Africa | 0 | 0 | 7 | 5 |
| Eastern Asia | 0 | 0 | 6 | 4.3 |
| Western Asia | 2 | 2.4 | 5 | 3.5 |
| Transnational | 0 | 0 | 9 | 6.4 |
| Total | 85 | 100 | 141 | 100 |

### *News Discourse*

Because startups function as a bridge between freelancers and legacy news media, the last part of this quantitative analysis measured news contextual discourse that freelancers relied on in producing different stories. In the study, the news discourse was conceptualized based on the geographical region of news events as well as the influence of news events in terms of geographical reach. Via this variable, the notion of global journalism could be tested in the stories produced by the freelancers. The test statistics indicated that freelancer-produced stories heavily focused on national event/national discourse (20, 23.5 percent) and transnational event/global discourse—full-fledged global journalism stories (19, 22.4 percent).

## Discussion and Conclusion

Globalization has opened new spaces—particularly digital spaces—in which global news startups operate. As "global challenges transcend local concerns and national systems, requiring transnational coordination and engagement to solve them" (Reese 2015, 2263), such global startups provide an important network to engage freelancers and reporters on the ground in global reporting. This engagement on a global level may offer new perspectives of foreign news innovation, and in particular, freelance journalism. As this study has shown, global news startups most likely emerged out of a need to organize resources digitally as well as the motivation to be innovative in global news. Freelancers may become the important deliverers of information in regard to global issues that transcend national boundaries. Furthermore, the mixed-methods results revealed how the global startups are typically engaged with freelancers and domestic journalists across the globe to serve their North American and Western European audiences. But while the startups aim to provide stories for a global audience, their clients are almost exclusively in Western countries. This might be a result of the crisis in the news industry in those particular countries.

By pairing the textual analysis of interviews with the content analysis of new stories published by Worldcrunch and ARA Network, it was possible to see a strong link between global discourse(s), clients served, and the news topics covered by Worldcrunch and ARA Network. The results revealed that most of the freelancer-produced stories focused on national event/national discourse and transnational event/global discourse. This was also supported by the textual analysis in which nearly all founders and editors mentioned

**TABLE 4**
Employment status of reporters covering stories for startups

| | ARA Network | | Worldcrunch | |
|---|---|---|---|---|
| **Employment status** | *N* | % | *N* | % |
| Domestic journalist | 9 | 10.6 | 79 | 56 |
| Freelancers | 63 | 74.1 | 22 | 15.6 |
| Foreign correspondent | 9 | 10.6 | 17 | 12.1 |
| Expert | 3 | 3.5 | 20 | 14.2 |
| Cannot be identified | 1 | 1.2 | 3 | 2.1 |
| Total | 85 | 100 | 141 | 100 |

**TABLE 5**
Geographical identity of main source in news stories

| | ARA Network (*N* = 85) | | Worldcrunch (*N* = 141) | |
|---|---|---|---|---|
| **Geographical identity** | *N* | % | *N* | % |
| North America | 7 | 8.2 | 6 | 4.3 |
| Central America | 2 | 2.4 | 2 | 1.4 |
| South America | 2 | 2.4 | 9 | 6.4 |
| Western Europe | 34 | 40 | 43 | 30.5 |
| East Europe | 4 | 4.7 | 3 | 2.1 |
| Africa | 10 | 11.8 | 9 | 6.4 |
| East Asia | 2 | 2.4 | 5 | 3.5 |
| South Asia | 3 | 3.5 | 0 | 0 |
| West Asia | 13 | 15.3 | 30 | 21.3 |
| Transnational actors | 2 | 2.4 | 8 | 5.7 |

that globalization has changed the client and audience expectations in terms of storytelling and hence has influenced startups to engage in more transnational and national discourses. The startups open a platform to be geographically and organizationally delocalized from a particular political and economic system. Hence, the way the stories are written is not dependent on a particular news organization but on the global outlook motivated by global news startups as intermediaries between freelance journalists and traditional media organizations.

In terms of news topics, there is also a dominance of geopolitics and terrorism in the news stories published by ARA Network and Worldcrunch, respectively (see Table 4). It is also clear that global issues and topics such as human rights, environment, and religion are frequently covered by these global startups. This argument is also consistent with the findings of the textual analysis in which interviewees mentioned how the news topics are more concerned with global issues crossing national boundaries. In an age when global news coverage is in retreat (Hammer 2014) and traditional Western news organizations have closed down their overseas bureaus and laid off experienced foreign correspondents due to the financial factors (Hammer 2014; Willmott 2010), freelancers have become a "cheaper solution" for legacy media to cover foreign news (Palmer 2015). With that said, global news startups may eventually serve as a changing force for freelance journalists to focus more on global issues within international reporting and journalistic storytelling.

Another important finding in the content analysis was the presence of news sources from Western Europe, North America, and Western Asia. This provides an important insight into the news events taking place during the sampling frame (November 2015 to February 2016). This included the Paris terrorist attacks, the threat posed by ISIS, as well as the refugee crisis in Syria and Western Europe, among others. These news events certainly fall into the time frame of the study and hence correlate with news topics covered by these global startups and the clients they served during that time frame. Nearly all the interviewees mentioned that North America appeared to be their major client, and this also explains the dominance of the English language in the startups' business model.

In terms of freelancers, the content analysis has shown that most of the stories incorporated either national or global discourses. This supports the argument that global journalism is increasingly through freelance labor and that freelancers are actually replacing the jobs of foreign correspondents in this particular type of global business model. On the whole, what stands is a lack of isomorphism among startups' business strategies: the startups have different business ideas and disagree whether editing stories should be part of global news startups' business content or should be left entirely to the traditional news organizations. Meanwhile, on an ideological level, all of the startups interviewed try to transcend national frames of reference and aim to build a global marketplace of news.

As the content analysis has revealed, the global frame may still be a goal rather than an actual reality. More efforts should be made to include languages other than English, or to reach out to regions where English is not the primary language and translate important stories that are happening there. However, some particular political systems may hinder such an expansion to global markets. This might also be one of the limitations of this study. The sampling process began by looking at academic publications and industry blogs. It was not possible to get overall statistics of global news startups around the world. The goal for future research is to conduct more studies on startups in regions other than the United States and Western Europe. Another limitation reflects one of the findings: the diversity of startups. Since not all startups actually edit their stories, it was only possible to analyze the stories of two startups. Based on the important findings, it seems relevant to discuss the outcome of such a digital global network of news production; hence, news stories are essential to understanding the building blocks of global journalism produced by the global news startups.

Most importantly, global journalism can transcend national frames of references and business models, contextualize motives, expose interconnectedness, and explore the scope of problems as well as human consequences (Cottle 2009). While commercial imperatives can conflict with journalistic values, these freelancers need to find a way to support their work if they are going to keep doing their jobs. International news is among the hardest to monetize, but research shows a positive relationship between the amount of hard international news coverage and citizens' level of foreign affairs knowledge. Media system differences may contribute to the perception of the importance of international news: whereas market-oriented media systems and broadcasters are less devoted to international news and focus more on soft than hard news (Aalberg et al. 2013), the situation is different in media systems with public broadcasting. Future studies should take into account how those dynamics play out in the construction of foreign news through startups to understand the merging or disconnect of media systems when it comes to global journalism.

## ACKNOWLEDGEMENTS

The authors would like to thank the founders of the global news startups for their time and insights and the reviewers for their very helpful feedback.

## DISCLOSURE STATEMENT

No potential conflict of interest was reported by the authors.

## NOTES

1. For an example of an online editorial desk and how startups work with news organizations, see http://www.ara-network.com/about-us/work-with-us/assign-us.html.
2. This refers to Middle Eastern countries. The development of geographical variables is based on the categories retrieved from the United Nations.

## REFERENCES


Aalberg, Toril, Stylianos Papathanassopoulos, Stuart Soroka, James Curran, Kaori Hayashi, Shanto Iyengar, Paul K. Jones, et al. 2013. "International TV News, Foreign Affairs Interest and Public Knowledge." *Journalism Studies* 14 (3): 387–406. doi:10.1080/1461670X.2013.765636.

Barth, Henrike, and Wolfgang Donsbach. 1992. "Aktivität und Passivität von Journalisten gegenüber Public Relations: Fallstudie am Beispiel von Pressekonferenzen zu Umweltthemen" [Activity and passivity of journalists in regards to public relations: A case study of press conferences on environmental themes]. *Publizistik* 37: 151–165.

Beck, Ulrich. 2005. *Power in the Global Age*. Cambridge, UK: Polity.

Bender, Bryan. 2014. "Perils Abound for Freelance Reporters in Hot Spots." *Boston Globe*, August 27. https://www.bostonglobe.com/news/nation/2014/08/27/heavy-reliance-freelancers-for-foreign-coverage-poses-challenges-for-media-and-greater-dangers/eMqwRsnBvwsPYFauWZnbgP/story.html.

Berglez, Peter. 2008. "What is Global Journalism? Theoretical and Empirical Conceptualizations." *Journalism Studies* 9 (6): 845–858.

Carlson, Matt, and Nikki Usher. 2015. "News Startups as Agents of Innovation." *Digital Journalism*. doi:10.1080/21670811.2015.1076344.

Committee to Protect Journalists. 2014. "International Journalists Killed at a High Rate in 2014: Middle East Deadliest Region for Press." https://cpj.org/reports/2014/12/international-journalists-killed-at-high-rate-in-2014-middle-east-deadliest-region-for-press.php.

Cottle, Simon. 2009. *Global Crisis Reporting: Journalism in the Global Age*. Berkshire, UK: Open University Press.

Deuze, Mark. 2005. "Popular Journalism and Professional Ideology: Tabloid Reporters and Editors Speak Out." *Media, Culture & Society* 27 (6): 861–882.

Dyer, John. 2014. "Have Laptop, Will Travel." *Nieman Reports* 68 (4): 32–37.

Edström, Maria, and Martina Ladendorf. 2012. "Freelance Journalists as a Flexible Workforce in Media Industries." *Journalism Studies* 6 (5): 711–721. doi:10.1080/17512786.2012.667275.

Hammer, Joshua. 2014. "Being There: The Escalating Personal and Financial Cost of Foreign Reporting is Changing the Way Correspondents Cover the World." *Nieman Reports* 68 (4): 22–29.

Hanitzsch, Thomas, and Karin Wahl-Jorgensen. 2009. "Introduction: On Why and How We Should Do Journalism Studies." In *The Handbook of Journalism Studies*, edited by Thomas Hanitzsch and Karin Wahl-Jorgensen, 3–16. New York: Routledge.

Lewis, Seth C., and Stephen D. Reese. 2009. "What is the War on Terror? Framing Through the Eyes of Journalists." *Journalism & Mass Communication Quarterly* 86 (1): 85–102.

Lewis, Seth C., and Nikki Usher. 2013. "Open Source and Journalism: Toward New Frameworks for Imagining News Innovation." *Media, Culture, & Society* 35 (5): 602–619.

Mahoney, Robert. 2015. "A Year After James Foley and Steven Sotloff Murders, More Awareness of Risks." *Committee to Protect Journalists*, August 17. https://cpj.org/blog/2015/08/a-year-after-james-foley-and-steven-sotloff-murder.php.

Meyen, Michael, and Nina Springer. 2009. *Freie Journalisten in Deutschland: Ein Report* [Freelance journalists in Germany: A report]. Konstanz, Germany: UVK Verlagsgesellschaft.

Morse, Janice M., and Linda Niehaus. 2009. *Mixed Method Design: Principles and Procedures*. Walnut Creek, CA: Left Coast Press.

Palmer, Lindsay. 2015. "Outsourcing Authority in the Digital Age: Television News Networks and Freelance War Correspondents." *Critical Studies in Media Communication* 32 (4): 225–239.

Paterson, Chris, and Annabelle Sreberny. 2004. *International News in the 21st Century*. Ann Arbor: University of Michigan Press.

Pew Research Center. 2014, March 26. "The Growth in Digital Reporting: What It Means for Journalism and News Consumers." http://www.journalism.org/files/2014/03/Shifts-in-Reporting_For-uploading.pdf.

Prosser, David. 2015. "How Freelancers are Taking Over the World." *Forbes*, June 24. Retrieved from http://www.forbes.com/sites/davidprosser/2015/06/24/how-freelancers-are-taking-over-the-world/#75c775de63a2.

Reese, Stephen D. 2008. "Theorizing a Globalized Journalism." In *Global Journalism Research: Theories, Methods, Findings, Future*, edited by Martin Loeffelholz and David Weaver, 240–252. London: Blackwell.

Reese, Stephen D. 2010. "Journalism and Globalization." *Sociology Compass* 4: 344–353. doi:10.1111/j.1751-9020.2010.00282.

Reese, Stephen D. 2015. "Globalization of Mediated Spaces: The Case of Transnational Environmentalism in China." *International Journal of Communication* 9: 2263–2281.

Reese, Stephen D. 2016. "The New Geography of Journalism Research." *Digital Journalism*. doi:10.1080/21670811.2016.1152903.

Ries, Eric. 2011. *The Lean Startup: How Today's Entrepreneurs Use Continuous Innovation to Create Radically Successful Businesses*. New York: Random House.

Riffe, Daniel, Stephen Lacy, and Frederick Fico, eds. 2014. *Analyzing Media Messages: Using Quantitative Content Analysis in Research*. New York: Routledge.

Ryan, Kathleen. 2009. "The Performative Journalist: Job Satisfaction, Temporary Workers, and American Television News." *Journalism* 10: 647–664.

Sassen, Saskia. 1996. "Losing Control? Sovereignty in an Age of Globalization." In *The 1995 Columbia University Leonard Hastings Schoff Memorial Lectures*. New York: Columbia University Press.

Shoemaker, Pamela J., and Stephen D. Reese. 2014. *Mediating the Message in the 21st Century: A Media Sociology Perspective*. New York: Routledge.

Shoemaker, Pamela J., and Tim P. Vos. 2009. *Gatekeeping Theory*. New York: Routledge.

Tashakkori, Abbas M., and Charles B. Teddlie. 2003. *Handbook of Mixed Methods in Social and Behavioral Research*. Thousand Oaks, CA: Sage.

Waisbord, Silvio, and Claudia Mellado. 2014. "De-Westernizing Communication Studies: A Reassessment." *Communication Theory* 24 (3): 361–372.

Willmott, Oliver. 2010. "The Decline of Foreign Correspondent." *New Statesman*, November 1. http://www.newstatesman.com/international-politics/2010/11/foreign-international-british.

# PAKISTANI GOVERNMENT–NEWS MEDIA RELATIONSHIPS

## How relevant are Western journalistic values?

**Nadeem Akhtar** and **Cornelius B. Pratt**

*This study investigates factors that contribute to the fraught relationships between the government and the news media in Pakistan. Responses from an online survey of 357 Pakistani journalists and educators indicate that (1) economic concerns are the focal point of government–news media relationships; (2) stiff competition among news organizations to provide platforms for government advertisements have affected journalistic standards; (3) higher government investment in advertisements resulted in governments receiving pro-government coverage; (4) private news media are coerced by the state through laws, regulations, licenses and taxes, leading to adversarial relationships between the news media and the government; (5) political affiliation, religion and national identity are the major influences on the journalists' worldviews; and (6) Western journalistic values do not seem to contribute significantly to developing universal journalistic values among Pakistani journalists in part because of cultural differences. The implications of these findings for journalism in Pakistan include having a better understanding of the plight of journalists and the media in that country and of the factors than can be considered to better improve government–media relationships.*

### Introduction

> Pakistani journalists are finding their voice after a long period of repression as their industry begins to take its place as a "fourth estate" that impacts … the body politic. While willing to challenge the government and the security forces, they see their primary task as explaining the complexities of Pakistani politics and society rather than overtly seeking political change.
> (Pintak and Syed 2013, 661)

Media autonomy and professionalism are major concerns of journalists globally—particularly of those in emerging economies and markets. One reason for such concerns is that they can ensure accountability of political systems and can promote national well-being. Journalists, on the one hand, are the voice of society and need to be shielded, as it were, from the suppressive policies of the government. On the other, they collaborate occasionally in helping implement government policies geared toward responding to the national interest. The absence of such social responsibility among journalists results in journalism that is moribund (Pratt and Akhtar 2013).

Pakistan's journalistic landscape is overridden by challenges that range from a lack of professionalism to ethical violations to physical threats to journalists. Pakistan has been ranked the third most dangerous country and the most dangerous democratic country in the world for journalists ("Top 10 Most Dangerous Places" 2015). Reporters Without Borders (2016) ranked Pakistan 147th out of 180 countries on the World Press Freedom Index. Similarly, Hofstede (2011) rated Pakistan as the world's most restrained country on the indulgence–restraint dimension, which means its citizens have minuscule opportunities to engage in a free expression of opinion and have little optimism about the future. Early in its history, write Pintak and Syed (2013, 641), "A succession of autocratic leaders kept the nation's news organizations on a tight leash … Today journalists are reveling in freedoms that seemed improbable a decade ago." Even so, government–news media relationships continue to be fraught with tensions. As Iqbal and Shabir (2010, 169) observed, "most of the time without any blunder on the part of the press or the presence of any extraordinary circumstances, the press had to encounter chains either in the shape of 'press advice system' or more impudent system of censorship." Particularly for private news media interests, it has been a perpetual culture of a constrained, fettered press, making it critical that national efforts be undertaken to establish stronger, better professional relationships among news organizations, journalists, and government agencies.

Nadadur (2007) cited four reasons for self-censorship among Pakistani journalists: (1) the unofficial government controls on reporting, (2) the oligopolistic newspaper ownership structure, (3) the legal system governing journalists, and (4) the lack of security for journalists. Shah (2015) reported that "corporate interests, political interference, and government attempts to regulate and censor information all put great strain on an institution still emerging from decades of oppression under military dictators."

Against the preceding background, the purpose of this article is fourfold. First, it explores government–news media relationships in the historical context; that is, it investigates how the media develop as an institution confronted by changing governments. The news media seek to promote awareness of government policies on health and education. Pintak and Syed (2013, 649), for example, noted that "Pakistani media's relationship with the government is not primarily one of the confrontations. Rather, there is a strong echo of the 'development journalism' of Southeast Asia, in which media and government partner for the good of the nation." There are also other terms that reflect "educate the public," "serve as a voice for the poor," and "transform society" (649). On the other hand, during a political campaign launched in March 2007 against President Musharraf to restore the judiciary, a lawyers movement, started in Karachi, Pakistan's largest city, as a long march to Islamabad, the nation's capital, used the slogan "Go Musharraf Go" as a threat to his presidency, forcing the president to impose emergency rule on November 3, 2007; to suspend the constitution; and to order a media blackout (Yamin 2015). In other words, the media sought to stimulate a public discourse on, as well as to counter, the government's media-suppression policies. Compagna (2007) acknowledges government's direct pressure on reporters and editors, noting its use of a variety of tactics to create journalistic barriers to media organizations.

Second, it investigates factors that can contribute to the testy relationships between the government and the media. Private media are mostly owned by business people or by politicians affiliated with a political party. During political crises, private media often play a divisive role in Pakistan ("Negative Facets of News Media" 2013; Pintak and Syed 2013).

Third, it argues that the challenges for Pakistan's professional journalists emanate from journalistic values unique to Pakistan's cultural and political landscape. Pintak and Syed (2013, 662) reported that "Pakistani journalists are carving out their own approach to the profession; shaping journalistic values born elsewhere to fit local culture, more and realities; aspiring to greater freedom and a higher level of professionalism." Even so, local and international media organizations such as the Pakistan Press Foundation and InterMedia are attempting to upgrade the professional standards of journalism in Pakistan (Ricchiardi 2012). Similarly, Internews (a US media-training organization) and Deutsche Welle (a German media-training organization) are imparting capacity-building skills on Pakistani journalists, in addition to linking with journalism schools in public universities. International fellowships are specifically offered to working journalists exposed to international media organizations and trained in Western journalistic values. International Media Support, a Danish-government supported organization, intends to provide technical, logistic, and institutional training and support for the Pakistani media through 2017 (Shah 2015). Even though the journalists are trained in journalistic ethics of the West, it is difficult to implement those values in local contexts when they return to their media institutions. Pintak and Syed (2013, 661) state that Pakistani journalists' "application of Western-style journalism norms are influenced by religion, nationalism and the economic realities of Pakistan."

Finally, this article argues that Pakistan's journalistic practices, unique to that nation, can serve as propositions for building a theory of emerging news media practices, even as a cadre of domestic, well-meaning journalists finds such practices inimical to their professional interests. In sum, this study applies the general theory of relationship management (e.g., Ledingham 2001, 2003; Ledingham and Bruning 1998; Strömbäck, Mitrook, and Kiousis 2010) to link government, media, and journalistic values, and to develop a model that will help build professional journalism in Pakistan without any deficiency/lack of trust between government and media organizations.

The media's role in Pakistan is to cover a range of issues from politics to social issues to social injustice, which can place journalists at a high risk of political and physical threats. The Committee to Protect Journalists (2016) reported that 58 journalists were killed between 1992 and 2016. Sixty-four percent of the victims were reporting politics, 38 percent war, 28 percent crime, 17 percent human-rights issues, 16 percent corruption, and the rest culture and business. In such circumstances, this study is significant in that it examines the relationship between government and the news media and the degree to which Western-style journalistic values influence Pakistani journalism. As Pakistan's news media push back on government constraints, the government is loosening its grip on media institutions. Former President Pervaz Musharraf, for example, encouraged the expansion of private media houses. Yet, when those same media supported the judiciary against the ex-president, he attempted to ban the voices of journalists through the Pakistan Electronic Media Regulatory Authority, which he established in 2002. Mazhar Abbas (2015) added that "successive governments tried to suppress the media and buy journalists instead of giving freedom to them." Similarly, in the current political turmoil, the media fall into two groups: Geo TV and Jang Group, both private news organizations which support government positions; and ARY, a private television news channel which exerts pressure on the government. Even though both media groups are privately owned, they have different approaches to reporting political turmoil, creating a multiplicity of divisive public opinions. Pintak and Syed (2014) reported that journalists and academics hold the view that the Pakistani media play a more divisive than an integrative role in society.

International nongovernmental organizations (NGOs) like Deutsche Welle and Internews attempt to empower Pakistani journalists by developing their technical skills and standardizing their journalistic ethics through various training sessions, providing yet another basis for the overarching importance of this study.

From a practical standpoint, this study presents evidence that governments and international NGOs can use to take stock of their understandings of the plight of journalists and media in Pakistan, to attempt to improve the relationship between government and the media, and to better understand the essence of journalism whenever it is influenced to some degree by universal standards applied to local contexts.

## Theoretical Framework: General Theory of Relationship Management (GTRM)

The crux of this article is media relations—both from the standpoint of the government and from that of news media organizations. Pakistani government public affairs specialists provide information to the public through platforms provided by both government and private news outlets and depend on the media for much of their publicity. Such a role should ordinarily be perceived in symmetrical terms; however, it is not uncommon for the news media to perceive uncooperativeness from and barriers by government agencies. The media need news on government to fill airtime and newspaper pages; government agencies need news channels and outlets to express their legitimacy and foster relationships with the public. This shared interest has been a bone of contention in Pakistan. Enter the general theory of relationship management (Hon and Grunig 1999; Huang 2001; Jo 2006; Ki and Hon 2007a, 2007b; Ledingham 2001, 2003; Ledingham and Bruning 1998; Strömbäck, Mitrook, and Kiousis 2010), which is presented here as the overarching theoretical framework for managing news media–government agency relationships and conflicts in Pakistan. Ledingham (2001) notes that GTRM emphasizes the importance of identifying and constructing exchanges that are based on shared interests and of measuring specific outcomes. It holds that publics expect mutuality in their relationships with an organization, and that it is this reciprocity, which occurs within the framework of relationship management, that sustains and nurtures a community relationship, which is related to personal relationships. Ledingham (2001, 292) writes, "When shared interests are the basis for public relations initiatives grounded in a commitment to mutual benefit, and when those initiatives are designed to accommodate differing interests, then community *can* be the result." Wilson (1994) describes it as a shift in management styles from the tradition of power and influence to corporate community-building, cooperative relationships, and relational responsibility, all of which are attainable in media–government relationships in Pakistan.

We draw upon three GTRM-related concepts—satisfaction, trust, and commitment—to provide insights for managing communicatively media–government relationships. All three concepts are rooted in the notion that communication, particularly its dialogic and negotiation components, is crucial to building relationships (Barnes 2001; Duncan and Moriarty 1998; Ki and Hon 2007a, 2007b; McKenzie 2001; Reichheld 2001; Shimp 2010; Temporal and Trott 2001), more so those associated with relationship marketing, which focuses on building relationships, networks, and interaction among various stakeholders and between them and organizations (Kodish and Pettegrew 2008). We shall now provide some depth on the three concepts in three subsections.

### *Defining Satisfaction, Trust, and Commitment*

Hon and Grunig (1999, 3) defined *satisfaction* as "[t]he extent to which each party feels favorably toward the other because positive expectations about the relationship are reinforced. A satisfying relationship is one in which the benefits outweigh the costs." Customer dissatisfaction, therefore, typically occurs when the risks to the customer are high and the benefits are minuscule.

*Trust* has had a variety of definitions: it is a commodity maintained and nurtured by relationships, accountability, credibility, and by the organizational systems in which transactions occur (Brown 2008; Dasgupta 1988); a communicative act (Luhmann 1979); and a product of confidence (Giddens 1990). Hon and Grunig (1999, 3), following Giddens, defined trust as "[o]ne party's level of confidence in and willingness to open oneself to the other party." They identified three dimensions of trust: integrity, dependability, and competence, all of which are vital to news media–government agency exchanges and with each to stakeholders. From the standpoint of relationship marketing, Morgan and Hunt (1994, 23) similarly conceptualize trust "as existing when one party has confidence in an exchange partner's reliability and integrity." Rotter (1967, 653), iterating both "dependability" and "reliability," defined trust as "a generalized expectancy that the oral or written statements of other people can be relied upon."

Hon and Grunig (1999, 3) define *commitment* as "[t]he extent to which each party believes and feels that the relationship is worth spending energy to maintain and promote." Employees of an organization, such as media staffers, will be committed to their organization in direct proportion to the benefits they get from it. It is correlated with job satisfaction (Meyer et al. 2002). Its dimensions are attitudinal or affective, continuance and normative. Affective, influenced by an individual's work and organizational experiences, is the depth of her or his identification and involvement with an organization; continuance is the perceived costs of leaving an organization; normative is the perceived obligation to remain in the organization (Hon and Grunig 1999; Meyer et al. 2002).

### *Distinguishing Among Trust, Confidence, and Distrust*

Luhmann (1979, 1988) makes a distinction between confidence and trust, noting that the former shows an absence of doubt whereas the latter is inherently linked to the awareness of risk, to uncertainty and anxiety (as in a global recession), to emotions, and to the absence of appropriate knowledge. Social theorists argue that interpersonal trust enables a people to manage the complexities and anxieties that are part of modern society (Giddens 1990; Luhmann 1988). The higher the investor's awareness of risk, the lower the confidence in the financial institution—and *vice versa*. A commonality between these two social phenomena is the nature of the action or inaction by a financial staffer. Absent communication that fosters institutional proximity to the client, the journalist remains abstruse to a government agency, undercutting any possibility for exchange and understanding on both sides and heightening the possibility among media users that either the government or the media organization or both do not support their best interests.

Such anxieties have been exacerbated by tense media–government relationships that engender crackdowns on the news media in the first place and that further erode the fragile confidence that customers had in both their governments and news media institutions.

Within the marketing communications context, trust is undermined when one party loses confidence in an exchange partner's integrity, dependability, and competence. Thus, when organizations engage in, or perpetuate, practices that undermine the essence of an amicable, professional news media–government agency relationship, marketing communications to manage a conflict are perceived as a Sisyphean task. Distrust is not necessarily the antonym of trust. As Welch (2006, 142) argued, rather than think about distrust "as a dangerous and destructive force, it might be more useful to consider it a natural state for discerning, prudent stakeholders who operate a sort of caveat emptor 'buyers beware' mechanism."

### *Identifying Trust as a Predictor*

Satisfaction by parties in a relationship is a strong, positive predictor of trust and trust is a strong predictor of commitment (Ki and Hon 2007a). Interestingly, when trust was controlled for in a path model, there was a significant but weak direct effect of satisfaction on commitment, indicating that organizations should go well beyond customer satisfaction if they want to have a constant stream of supporters and to expand their operations, a finding supported by earlier research (Hon and Grunig 1999; Huang 2001; Jo 2006). All three constructs, as global measures of organization (newspapers)–public (government) relationships (Jo 2006), can be instrumental in addressing the everyday anxieties that stem from tensions in government–media relationships, particularly as they relate to Pakistan's journalistic landscape.

### *Research Questions*

**RQ1:** How do Pakistani journalists and educators perceive government–media relationships within the context of media criticism or media support of the government?

**RQ2:** What factors affect journalists' opinions of journalistic work in Pakistan?

**RQ3:** Do Western-style journalistic values contribute to developing universal journalistic values among Pakistani journalists? If so, to what degree do they contribute to amicable government–media relationships?

**RQ4:** What propositions for theory building on the news media environment of an emerging economy do the cumulative findings of this present study suggest?

## Method

### *Questionnaire Design*

A two-part questionnaire was developed and content-validated to determine and analyze factors responsible for government–news media relationships in Pakistan. Part I comprised 24 items anchored on a five-point, Likert-type scale. Eight items in Part I sought information on respondents' demographics.

### *Sampling*

The sample comprised journalists and journalism educators working in a variety of private and government media organizations. All participants had been trained in Pakistan or overseas through various programs offered by agencies such as the United States Agency for International Development and by international NGOs such as Internews, Deutsche Welle, and InterMedia. These international NGOs also assisted the authors by providing access to journalists and journalism educators who had been trained in different media streams.

A four-page questionnaire was administered electronically to 436 practicing journalists and journalism educators in spring 2016. Prospective respondents were invited through e-mail messages and personal telephone calls to complete the questionnaire. Because most of the journalists were also members of press clubs, they were also contacted through their presidents, who helped identify target journalists. Three hundred and fifty-seven participants provided usable responses, for an 82 percent response rate.

### *Statistical Analysis*

*t*-Test and correlation and regression analyses were used in data analyses. An independent sample *t*-test was conducted to determine the respondents' perceptions of government–news media relationships and the differences between the means of two groups' (journalists and educators) perceptions of government–media relationships. In addition, correlation analysis was used to discover the strength and direction of the relationships between the variables. The effects of independent variables (molding media content, controlling media by government, coercing private media, depriving critical media outlets, enforcing press laws on media houses, accepting government orders, and interfering in free expression) on the dependent variable, government–news media adversarial relationship, were determined through regression analysis.

## Findings and Discussion

Nearly two-thirds of the respondents were male, 36 percent female. About 67 percent of them served in private electronic or print media organizations while about one-third were journalism educators in various private or public institutions.

### *Findings on RQ1*

How do Pakistani journalists and educators perceive government–media relationships within the context of media criticism or media support of the government?

Results in Table 1, column 1, on whether owners and journalists are perceived to be on the same page, indicate that there is no significant difference between the mean scores for journalists (mean = 2.1552) and those for educators (mean = 2.3818). Both groups, journalists and educators, tend to disagree with the statement that media owners and journalists are on the same page; however, journalists tend to disagree slightly more than do educators. One reason could be that it is the media owners who develop policies and expect journalists to follow them. Nadadur's (2007) results also support our argument. Column 2 of Table 1 also shows that there is no significant difference between the mean

**TABLE 1**

Mean score differences between Pakistani journalists ($N = 116$) and educators ($N = 55$) on 12 government–news media variables

| | 1 Owners and journalists on same page | 2 Govt. media control | 3 Media economic concerns | 4 Ads and government suppression | 5 Private media coerced | 6 Molding public opinion | 7 Critical outlets deprived | 8 Govt. relate to coverage | 9 Molding media content | 10 Laws and media houses | 11 Govt. agencies and media freedom | 12 Govt. ads and journalistic standards |
|---|---|---|---|---|---|---|---|---|---|---|---|---|
| Overall | 2.2685 | 3.9912 | 3.5644 | 2.5857 | 4.126 | 3.9085 | 3.4832 | 3.7179 | 3.5910 | 3.0594 | 3.8496 | 3.6630 |
| Journalists | 2.1552 | 3.9914 | 3.1379 | 3.1897 | 4.3793 | 3.8534 | 3.9483 | 3.8448 | 3.3276 | 3.1552 | 3.8448 | 3.6897 |
| Educators | 2.3818 | 3.9091 | 3.9091 | 1.9818 | 3.8727 | 3.9636 | 3.0182 | 3.5091 | 3.8545 | 2.9636 | 3.8545 | 3.6364 |
| *T* | −1.445 | 0.802 | −4.889** | 12.618** | 6.247** | −2.088* | 4.418** | 1.725* | −4.982** | 1.447 | −0.147 | 0.404 |

1. Media owners and journalists are on the same page.
2. Government controls media through advertisements and other incentives.
3. The primary concerns of the media in Pakistan are economic rather than political.
4. Through advertising, the government is powerful enough to suppress media outlets it wants to.
5. In Pakistan, the private media channels are coerced by the state through laws, regulations, licenses, and taxes.
6. Media owners and journalists are bribed at times by government to mold public opinion.
7. Media outlets critical of government policies are deprived of government advertisements.
8. The higher the amount of government advertisements placed in the media, the higher the pro-government coverage.
9. Government is influential in molding media content.
10. Press laws and government ordinances are being adhered to by government and media houses.
11. Government agencies interfere with journalists' freedom of expression.
12. The race to procure government advertisements has affected journalistic standards in the country.

Mean scores were calculated on a five-point scale: 1 = strongly disagree; 5 = strongly agree.

*$p < 0.05$, **$p < 0.01$.

scores for journalists (mean = 3.9914) and those for educators (mean = 3.9091) in their perceptions of government control of media through advertisements and other incentives. It is also argued here that the absence of a shared interest has the potential to exacerbate tense government–media relationships. Journalists think the primary interest of media owners is pecuniary; for the journalists themselves, it is professionalism. The theory of relationship management posits that the lack of satisfaction can result in distrust of an organization, an outcome that can ultimately affect the commitment of news staffers to professional values. Journalists might not be satisfied with what they perceive as a singular focus of media owners on an economic model of news operations to the degree that such an approach is antithetical to the professional values of journalism, even as it is practiced in Pakistan's muffled, fettered environment. Ali (2016, 464) noted that "Geo TV is a private media organization, so it might be more governed by the consideration of market economy than by services to the society." It behooves media owners, then, to take stock of the effects of their values and whether they undermine the very essence of the professionalism of journalism in an emerging economy. As Strömbäck and Karlsson (2011) explain, media owners plan budgets, devise editorial guidelines and policies, recruit reporters and managerial staff, and thus affect the process of news production overall. It means that journalists have no independent role and they have to develop the stories in accordance with their owners' policies and affiliations.

Further, Table 1, column 3 indicates that there is a statistically significant difference between the mean scores for journalists (mean = 3.1379) and educators (mean = 3.9091). The results further suggest that educators tend to have a stronger agreement than journalists with the notion that the media establishment (read: the media owner) is more interested in ensuring its economic survival and profit-making than in engaging in journalism *per se*. This is analogous to issues raised by checkbook journalism in the United States (e.g., Boynton 2008) and by brown-envelope journalism in developing economies (e.g., Gokah, Dzokoto, and Ndiweni 2009), and it supports the perception that media owners and journalists are clearly not on the same page. Additionally, results in Table 1, column 4, indicate significantly stronger agreement among journalists (mean = 3.1897) than among educators (mean = 1.9818) with the statement on government's controlling media outlets through placement of advertisements. These results are consistent with Nadadur's (2007, 50) findings, which indicated that Pakistani newspaper owners "are more concerned with their business interests rather than with a free press; their economic interests lie in promoting government interests." He argued that "because owners of newspapers have monopolistic influence over journalists' job security and wages, journalists are forced to succumb to the desires of the owners" (51). Memon (2015) offers an additional insight into government–press relationships: that policies of media organizations depend on the latter's relationships with government and that journalists are merely the sandwich between the two organizations.

Results in Table 1, column 5, also indicate that journalists have significantly stronger agreement (mean = 4.3793) than educators (mean = 3.8727) that the private media are coerced by the state through its laws, regulations, licenses, and taxes, leading to adversarial relationships between the news media and the government. A plausible reason for this outcome could be that because journalists tend to operate from the trenches, they are more susceptible than educators to—and have a more direct experience with—government machinations aimed at nurturing a docile media system. Results in column 6 indicate that educators (mean = 3.9636) agree significantly more than journalists (mean = 3.8534) that government molds public opinion through media by bribing media owners and journalists. One example of this trend is highlighted by the *Express Tribune* ("Secret Funds Case" 2013), a widely known English-language newspaper, which stated that "[j]ournalists and members of the civil society demanded the Supreme Court make public the names of the private TV channel that received Rs300 million from the information ministry and of all those journalists who allegedly received huge payments from the ministry." Additionally, the organizational relationship is based mainly on trust, which seems absent in government–news media relationships in Pakistan. One of the reasons is that private media are largely owned by business interests and by politicians whose agendas tend to be self-centered and individualistic. But, more important, such agendas perpetuate social divisiveness and political turmoil (e.g., "Negative Facets of News Media" 2013; Pintak and Syed 2013).

Similarly, journalists perceive government advertisements, media laws, regulations, licenses, and taxes as vehicles through which the government seeks to control the media and their freedom of expression. Results in Table 1, columns 7 and 8, show significant differences between the mean scores of journalists and educators, suggesting that journalists take a less optimistic view than educators. Such perceptions of the media organizations have the potential to create (professional) dissatisfaction among the journalists who believe that following such media policies is a disservice to upholding the standards of journalism and that both government and news media organizations are equally responsible for such an outcome. It seems plausible, then, that because media owners are more concerned with monetary benefits, they are usually not as committed to national causes as governments tend to be. Table 1, column 9, shows that educators (mean = 3.8545) have stronger agreement than journalists (mean = 3.3276) on government as influential in molding media content. One argument in this regard is that educators are more critical than media practitioners and thus can analyze how the government molds media content. In contrast, results in columns 10–12 show that there are no significant differences in the mean scores of journalists and educators and that both groups believe strongly that the press laws and government ordinances are being adhered to by the government and media houses, that government agencies interfere with journalists' freedom of expression, and that the competition to get as much government advertising as possible has affected journalistic standards, creating distrust, dissatisfaction, and less commitment to the news organization. In relationship management, organizations should demonstrate primary responsibility to all stakeholders. Absent that social responsibility, relationships among principals in media organizations—owners, news staffers, news media audiences—will become fraught.

### *Findings on RQ2*

What factors affect journalists' opinions of journalistic work in Pakistan?

A correlation analysis was undertaken to explore factors that significantly affect journalists' opinions of journalistic work in Pakistan. The correlation analysis (Table 2) shows significant positive associations between the following variables:

- government media control and (1) media's adversarial relationships ($r = 0.112$, $p < 0.05$); and (2) media influence on political opinion ($r = 0.532$, $p < 0.01$);
- private media being coerced through laws and regulations and (1) media's adversarial relationships ($r = 0.317$, $p < 0.01$); (2) the media's influence on political opinion

**TABLE 2**

Regression of media adversarial relationships on independent variables ($N = 357$)

| | Constant | 1 Government media control | 2 Molding media content | 3 Private media coerced | 4 Critical outlets deprived | 5 Press laws and the media | 6 Government orders and the media acceptance | 7 Government agencies and the freedom of expression |
|---|---|---|---|---|---|---|---|---|
| Coefficient | 1.797*** | −0.374*** | 0.117* | 0.113** | −0.280*** | 0.204*** | 0.224*** | 0.371*** |
| $t$ | 7.675 | −6.959 | 2.121 | 2.466 | −6.269 | 4.878 | 4.397 | 7.247 |
| $R^2 = 0.458$, $F(7, 349) = 42.126$*** | | | | | | | | |

1. Government controls media through advertisements and other incentives.
2. Government is influential in molding media content.
3. In Pakistan, the private media channels are coerced by the state through laws, regulations, licenses, and taxes.
4. Media outlets critical of government policies are deprived of government advertisements.
5. Press laws and government ordinances are being adhered to by government and media houses.
6. The media toe the government line by accepting government orders.
7. Government agencies interfere with journalists' freedom of expression.

*$p < 0.05$, **$p < 0.01$, ***$p < 0.001$.

($r = 0.347$, $p < 0.01$); and (3) government's media controls through advertisements and other incentives ($r = 0.354$, $p < 0.01$);

- government advertisements deprived of news organizations and (1) media role in influencing political opinion ($r = 0.260$, $p < 0.01$); and (2) government's media control through advertisements and other incentives ($r = 0.299$, $p < 0.01$);
- press laws and promulgation of ordinance that are being adhered to by the government and media houses and (1) media's adversarial relationships ($r = 0.246$, $p < 0.01$); and (2) deprivation of government advertisements ($r = 0.285$, $p < 0.01$);
- news media's toeing the government line by accepting government orders and (1) media's adversarial relationships ($r = 0.437$, $p < 0.01$); (2) media role in influencing political opinion ($r = 0.195$, $p < 0.01$); (3) government's media control through advertisements and other incentives ($r = 0.285$, $p < 0.01$); (4) coercion of private media through laws and regulations ($r = 0.241$, $p < 0.01$); (5) deprivation of government advertisements ($r = 0.339$, $p < 0.01$); and (6) promulgation of ordinance and press laws that are being adhered to by the government and media houses ($r = 0.208$, $p < 0.01$);
- government agencies' interference with journalists' freedom of expression and (1) media's adversarial relationships ($r = 0.398$, $p < 0.01$); (2) media role in influencing political opinion ($r = 0.267$, $p < 0.01$); (3) government's media controls through advertisements and other incentives ($r = 0.457$, $p < 0.01$); (4) coercion of private media through laws and regulations ($r = 0.473$, $p < 0.01$); (5) deprivation of government advertisements ($r = 0.210$, $p < 0.01$); (6) promulgation of ordinance and press laws are being adhered to by the government and media houses ($r = 0.135$, $p < 0.01$); and (7) media toe the government line by accepting government orders ($r = 0.355$, $p < 0.01$).

Correlation analysis (Table 2) shows only one significant negative association: media adherence to press laws and government ordinance correlated negatively with media role in influencing political opinion ($r = -0.215$, $p < 0.01$) (Table 3). Additionally, correlation analysis (Table 4) shows significant positive associations between the following variables:

- the economic priorities of the state have changed the infrastructure of the media industry in Pakistan and the primary focus of media in Pakistan is economic rather than political ($r = 0.640$, $p < 0.05$); and
- the higher the number of government advertisements placed in the media, the higher will be the frequency of pro-government coverage and (1) the primary focus of media in Pakistan is economic rather than political ($r = 0.308$, $p < 0.05$); and (2) the economic priorities of the state have changed the infrastructure of the media industry in Pakistan ($r = 0.297$, $p < 0.05$).

Results on RQ1 and RQ2 indicate that monetary concerns are a reason for the divide between journalists and media owners and for the adversarial relationships between them. Put differently, monetary transactions between media owners and the government define the relationships between them; journalists' professionalism is constrained in that process. As stated in a preceding paragraph, in Pakistan, the focus of that relationship is economic, not political. This finding indicates that the more monetary benefits media organizations get from the government, the higher will be the pro-government coverage. These results further intensify the perception that economic concerns are the main driving force of

ation coefficients for media adversarial relationships with government ($N = 357$)

| | 1 Media adversarial relationship | 2 Media influence on political opinion | 3 Government controls media | 4 Private media coerced | 5 Critical outlets deprived | 6 Press laws and the media | 7 Government orders and the media acceptance | Gove and |
|---|---|---|---|---|---|---|---|---|
| ial | 1 | | | | | | | |
| e on ion | −0.067 | 1 | | | | | | |
| ntrols | 0.112* | 0.532** | 1 | | | | | |
| oerced | 0.317** | 0.347** | 0.354** | 1 | | | | |
| | −0.070 | 0.260** | 0.299** | 0.081 | 1 | | | |
| the | 0.246** | −0.215** | 0.016 | 0.094 | 0.285** | 1 | | |
| ders ia | 0.437** | 0.195** | 0.285** | 0.241** | 0.339** | 0.208** | 1 | |
| encies lom of | 0.398** | 0.267** | 0.457** | 0.473** | 0.210** | 0.135* | 0.355** | 1 |

ave adversarial relationships with the government.
nce political opinion.
controls media through placing advertisements and by offering other incentives.
he private media channels are coerced by the state through laws, regulations, licenses, and taxes.
s critical of government policies are deprived of government advertisements.
nd government ordinances are being adhered to by government and media houses.
e the government line by accepting government orders.
agencies interfere with journalists' freedom of expression.
$< 0.01$.

**TABLE 4**
Pearson correlation coefficients for government–news media relationships *vis-à-vis* economic concerns ($N = 357$)

| | 1 Media concerns | 2 State economic priorities and the media | 3 Government relate to coverage |
|---|---|---|---|
| Media concerns | 1 | | |
| State economic priorities and the media | 0.640** | 1 | |
| Government relate to coverage | 0.308** | 0.297** | 1 |

1. The primary focus of media in Pakistan is economic rather than political.
2. Economic priorities of the state have changed the infrastructure of the media industry in Pakistan.
3. The higher the number of government advertisements placed in the media, the higher will be the pro-government coverage.

**$p < 0.01$.

amicable or adversarial relationships between media and the government. Correlation results clearly indicate that economic concerns of media are a push–pull factor in developing a pro- or an anti-government relationship.

We tested these relationships in regression models. Table 2 shows a significant regression equation model ($F(7, 349) = 42.126$, $p < 0.001$, $R^2 = 0.458$). The results also indicate that the use of government tactics to control media through advertisements, rules, and regulations ($\beta = 0.113$, $t(356) = 2.466$, $p < 0.001$); and government agencies' interference with journalists' freedom of expression ($\beta = 0.371$, $t(356) = 7.247$, $p < 0.001$) are key factors in whether the media develop cordial or adversarial relationships with governments, and, by extension, whether the professionalism of news staffers is grounded in practices that respond to the nation's best interest.

Similarly, in Table 5, the respondents also indicate that favorable government coverage is important for procuring government advertisements ($\beta = 0.129$, $t(356) = 3.062$, $p < 0.01$), a practice that might affect journalistic standards and determine the amicable or adversarial stance of the government in its relationship with the media. A significant model was developed ($F(2, 354) = 130.999$, $p < 0.001$, $R^2 = 0.425$).

**TABLE 5**
Regression of media economic concerns on media infrastructure and pro-government coverage in Pakistan ($N = 357$)

| | Constant | 1 State economic priorities and the media | 2 Government relate to coverage |
|---|---|---|---|
| Standardized coefficient | 0.212 | 0.602*** | 0.129** |
| $t$ | 0.912 | 14.265 | 3.062 |
| $R^2 = 0.425$, $F(2, 354) = 130.999$*** | | | |

1. Economic priorities of the state have changed the infrastructure of the media industry in Pakistan.
2. The higher the number of government advertisements placed in the media, the higher will be the pro-government coverage.

**$p < 0.01$, ***$p < 0.001$.

A significant model ($F(6, 351) = 74.590$, $p < 0.001$, $R^2 = 0.515$) in Table 6 illustrates that the training offered by the international NGOs in Western-style journalistic values, which can contribute to developing universal journalistic values among Pakistani journalists, cannot come to fruition ($\beta = -0.161$, $t(354) = -3.914$, $p < 0.001$) unless true professionalism is developed among the media owners in the first place. These owners are the formidable driving forces of journalistic practices in Pakistan. The regression results indicate that government advertisements ($\beta = 0.510$, $t(354) = 9.956$, $p < 0.001$) and coercion on private media through laws and regulations ($\beta = -0.258$, $t(354) = -6.313$, $p < 0.001$) are two key factors that influence the standards of journalism in Pakistan. The results also show that the two organizations (that is, the media and the government) have weak relationships *vis-à-vis* economic priorities. In addition, the results further suggest that these fraught relationships between government and the news media are based on the changing levels of trust and distrust because of political turmoil over time. Such results resonate with GTRM, which emphasizes that trust is one of the key factors conducive to having effective communication between the two organizations (Welch 2006).

### *Findings on RQ3*

Do Western-style journalistic values contribute to developing universal journalistic values among Pakistani journalists? If so, to what degree do they contribute to amicable government–media relationships?

Even though all respondents were trained by Internews (a US media-training organization), Deutsche Welle (a German media-training organization), or similar organizations, Table 7 shows that there are significant differences between the mean scores for journalists (mean = 3.2759) and educators (mean = 3.6000). A plausible reason for the significantly higher agreement among educators could be that their approach is more idealistic whereas journalists practicing their craft in the trenches are exposed to realities that

**TABLE 6**

Regression of the affected journalistic standards on independent variables ($N = 357$)

| | Constant | 1 Owners/ journalists on same page | 2 Private media coerced | 3 Critical outlets deprived | 4 Government relates to coverage | 5 Western style values and practices |
|---|---|---|---|---|---|---|
| Standardized coefficient | 2.873*** | −0.154*** | −0.258*** | 0.239*** | 0.510*** | −0.161*** |
| *t* | 10.552 | −3.777 | −6.313 | 4.746 | 9.956 | −3.914 |
| $R^2 = 0.515$, $F(6, 351) = 74.590$*** | | | | | | |

1. Media owners and journalists are on the same page.
2. In Pakistan, the private media channels are coerced by the state through laws, regulations, licenses and taxes.
3. Media outlets critical of government policies are deprived of government advertisements.
4. The higher the number of government advertisements placed in the media the higher will be the pro-government coverage.
5. Western-style journalistic values are not influencing local journalistic practices because of cultural differences.

***$p < 0.001$.

**TABLE 7**

Journalists' ($N = 116$) and educators' ($N = 55$) mean scores on three Western-style journalistic values

| | Western-style journalistic values contribute to developing universal journalistic values | Western-style journalistic values contribute to developing amicable government–media relationships | Western-style journalistic values do not influence local journalistic practices because of cultural differences |
|---|---|---|---|
| Overall | 3.4379 | 3.1608 | 3.0868 |
| Journalists | 3.2759 | 3.1034 | 3.4828 |
| Educators | 3.6000 | 3.2182 | 2.6909 |
| *t* | −2.557* | −1.247 | 7.377** |

$^{*}p < 0.05$, $^{**}p < 0.01$.

could threaten their adopting such values. Further, there is no significant difference between journalists and educators on the statement that Western-style journalistic values contribute to developing amicable government–media relationships. Finally, the degree that monetary concerns are the main reason for amicable or adversarial relationships between the media and the government in Pakistan imply that Western values are not likely to guide the actual practice of journalism in Pakistan.

### *Findings on RQ4*

What propositions for theory-building on the news media environment of an emerging economy do the cumulative findings of this study suggest?

Pakistan's journalism, as a social institution, is a logical product of its culture—politically and socially—regardless of the exposure to Western journalistic practices that its journalists may have had—or continue to have. Even when Pakistani journalists seek to practice aspects of Western journalistic values, they might feel constrained in their attempt to parlay such experiences into everyday journalism in their home country. In addition, Table 7 also indicates, on the one hand, that there is a significant difference between the mean scores of journalists (mean = 3.4828) and those for educators (mean = 2.6909). Journalists, as practitioners, believe that Western-style journalistic values do not influence local journalistic practices because of cultural differences. On the other, educators believe that Western-style journalistic values contribute to developing universal journalistic values among Pakistani journalists. Both these findings acknowledge the perceived relevance of Western values to Pakistan's journalistic practices. Therefore, we present the following propositions (P1–P4):

**P1:** Pakistani journalists will not subscribe to Western journalistic values because of the constrained professional environment in which they operate and the difficulties in applying such values to or enacting them in their home country.

**P2:** To increase their professional impact on the everyday practice of Pakistani journalism, Pakistani journalists should deepen their professionalism in balancing Western and home-country values particularly as they relate to the circumstances of an emerging economy.

**P3:** Pakistani journalists will perceive collaborations with government agencies and media owners as relationship indicators in a coalition of professionals with a common national interest in ensuring clarity of expectations and in contributing collectively to managing the nation's challenges.

This study raises issues of government coercion and control and of the economic knock-on effects of media criticism of government policies. From a theoretical standpoint, constructs embedded in the two 3s (that is, three dimensions each of trust and of commitment) and satisfaction can serve as countervailing forces in creating the professional environment conducive to accomplishing functional journalism in an emerging economy and to fulfilling its primary responsibility of "explaining the complexities of Pakistani politics and society rather than overtly seeking political change" (Pintak and Syed 2013, 661). The point here is to increase satisfaction, trust (integrity, dependability, and competence) and commitment (affective, normative, and continuance) among the three stakeholders (journalists, media owners, and government), thereby enhancing Pakistan's journalistic professionalism and its social responsibility in the long run. This leads to the final proposition:

**P4:** Satisfaction, trust, and commitment, hallmarks of productive relationships among journalists, media owners and government operatives, will be valued in Pakistan as a desideratum for building and strengthening functional journalism as development journalism in an emerging economy.

All four propositions, when tested empirically, could be the foundation for building a theory of emerging news media practices: that the vibrancy of a local culture—politically and socially—serves as an enabling agent in ensuring a journalistic environment as sensitive and adaptive to local practices as it is to relevant Western journalistic practices.

## Conclusions and Implications for Public Policymaking

The objective of this study was to investigate the importance of government–news media relationships in Pakistan. Given the opacity of Pakistan's government, it is little wonder that the relationships between it and the news media are fraught. The nation's media organizations continue to face mounting challenges: sensationalism, anti-democratic press, media laws and regulations, the paucity of trained journalists, and minuscule professionalism (Pratt and Akhtar 2013; Ramaprasad 2013). Ramaprasad (2013) further notes that today's Pakistani media are comparatively free but media control still exists in the form of regulations, government advertisements, and access to military and political news sources. Dickinson and Memon (2012) report that in spite of critical press–government relations, there is open criticism and political debate in newspapers. The challenges of Pakistan's journalism "undermine its social influence and informational impact" (Pratt and Akhtar 2013, 129).

The results of this study of a convenience sample of Pakistani journalists and journalism educators contribute to the literature on journalism in emerging nations, particularly in an attempt to begin establishing the groundwork for understanding the essence of journalism whenever it is influenced to some degree by universal standards of the practice, as applied to local contexts. An answer to a key question posed by this study is that Western-style journalism has a minimal effect on Pakistani journalism in which culture and economics play an outsize role, leading to fraught relationships between media owners and news staffers. Some 75 percent of the journalists say that their religion, political affiliation, and national identity influence their worldviews, which have the potential to enable journalists to question the appropriateness of the influence of Western-style journalistic values on them. It is important, then, that any national efforts toward policymaking aimed at addressing the challenges and experiences of Pakistani journalists acknowledge the role of religion, politics, and national identity as both enabling and disabling factors of the country's journalistic landscape.

This study also finds that media economic concerns and government's efforts to control the media through government advertisements, incentives, and government agencies' interferences with journalists' freedom of expression through laws and regulations are the main driving factors that determine the presence of amicable or adversarial relationships between the government and the media. The international NGOs' contributions to developing Western-style journalistic values among Pakistani journalists and to contributing to universal journalistic values cannot be expected to take root in their entirety until the push–pull factors identified in this study are addressed head on by the media organizations themselves and by the government, particularly in light of the aversion among Pakistani journalists toward enacting Western journalistic standards in their home country.

## DISCLOSURE STATEMENT

No potential conflict of interest was reported by the authors.

## FUNDING

A project titled "Culture Fusion of Enterprises" with a grant ID is 2014WGJHZ001 was sponsored by Guangdong Public Diplomacy and Intercultural Communication Research Center for this research.

## REFERENCES

Abbas, Mazhar. 2015. "Media Ethics, Safety: Government, Media Owners Urged to Work in Concert." *The Express Tribune*, January 30. http://tribune.com.pk/story/829929/media-ethics-safety-government-media-owners-urged-to-work-in-concert/.

Ali, Zulfiqar. 2016. "Pakistan, Military Coup, and Concordance: Four Objections to Schiff." *Armed Forces and Society* 42 (2): 463–469.

Barnes, James G. 2001. *Secrets of Customer Relationship Management: It's all about how you make them Feel*. New York: McGraw-Hill.

Boynton, Robert S. 2008. "Checkbook Journalism Revisited: Sometimes we owe our Sources Everything." *Columbia Journalism Review* 46 (5): 12–14.

Brown, Patrick R. 2008. "Trusting the New NHS: Instrumental versus Communicative Action." *Sociology of Health & Illness* 30: 349–363.

Campagna, Joel. 2007. "Attacks on the Press 2007: Pakistan. https://cpj.org/2008/02/attacks-on-the-press-2007-pakistan.php.

Committee to protect journalists. 2016. "58 Journalists Killed in Pakistan since 1992/motive Confirmed." https://www.cpj.org/killed/asia/pakistan/.

Dasgupta, Partha. 1988. "Trust as a Commodity." In *Trust: Making and Breaking Cooperative Relations*, edited by Diego Gambetta, 49–72. Oxford: Basil Blackwell.

Dickinson, Roger, and Bashir Memon. 2012. "Press Clubs, the Journalistic Field and the Practice of Journalism in Pakistan." *Journalism Studies* 13 (4): 616–632. doi:10.1080/1461670X.2011.629109.

Duncan, Tom, and E. Sandra Moriarty. 1998. "A Communication-based Marketing Model for Managing Relationships." *Journal of Marketing,* 62 (2): 1–13.

Giddens, Anthony. 1990. *The Consequences of Modernity*. Palo Alto, CA: Stanford University Press.

Gokah, Theophilus K., Percival K. Dzokoto, and Esinath E. Ndiweni. 2009. "Brown Envelope Journalism, Policing the Policeman, Conflict of Interest and (Media) Corporate Governance: The case of Ghana." *International Journal of Disclosure and Governance* 6 (2): 167–179.

Hofstede, Geert. 2011. "*Culture's Continuing Consequences*." Paper presented at the Asia Service Business Research Institute, Waseda University, Tokyo, June.

Hon, Linda C., and James E. Grunig. 1999. *Guidelines for Measuring Relationships in Public Relations*. Gainesville, FL: Institute for Public Relations.

Huang, Yi-Hui. 2001. "OPRA: A Cross-cultural, Multiple-item Scale for Measuring Organization-public relationships." *Journal of Public Relations Research* 13: 61–90.

Iqbal, Zafar, and Ghulam Shabir. 2010. "Press-government Relations in Structural-functionalist Perspective: A case of Pakistan under General Zia (from 1977 to 1988)." *Pakistan Journal of Social Sciences* 30: 167–179.

Jo, Samsup. 2006. "Measurement of Organization-public Relationship: Validation of Measurement Using a Manufacturer-retailer Relationship." *Journal of Public Relations Research* 18: 225–248.

Ki, Eyun-Jung, and Linda C. Hon. 2007a. "Testing the Linkage among the Organization-public Relationship and Attitude and Behavioral Intentions." *Journal of Public Relations Research* 19: 1–23.

Ki, Eyun-Jung, and Linda C. Hon. 2007b. "Reliability and Validity of Organization-public Relationship Measurement and Linkages among Relationship Indicators in a Membership Organization." *Journalism & Mass Communication Quarterly* 84: 419–438.

Kodish, Slavia, and Loyd S. Pettegrew. 2008. "Enlightened Communication is the Key to Building Relationships." *Journal of Relationship Marketing* 7: 151–176.

Ledingham, John A. 2001. "Government-community Relationships: Extending the Relational Theory of Public relations." *Public Relations Review* 27: 285–295.

Ledingham, John A. 2003. "Explicating Relationship Management as a General Theory of Public Relations." *Journal of Public Relations Research* 15: 181–198.

Ledingham, John A., and Stephen D. Bruning. 1998. "Relationship Management in Public Relations: Dimensions of an Organization-public Relationship." *Public Relations Review* 24 (1): 55–65.

Luhmann, Niklas. 1979. *Trust and Power*. Chichester: Wiley.

Luhmann, Niklas. 1988. "Familiarity, Confidence, Trust: Problems and Alternatives." In *Trust: Making and Breaking Cooperative Relations*, edited by Diego Gambetta, 94–108. Oxford, UK: Basil Blackwell.

McKenzie, Ray. 2001. *The Relationship Based Enterprise: Powering Business Success Through Customer Relationship Management*. Toronto: McGraw-Hill/Ryerson.

Memon, Bashir. 2015. "Policy of Media Owners/organizations and Governments Towards Journalists in Pakistan." *The Government: Research Journal of Political Science Supplementary Edition* 3 (3): 51–66.

Meyer, John P., David J. Stanley, Lynne Herscovitch, and Laryssa Topolnytsky. 2002. "Affective, Continuance, and Normative Commitment to the Organization: A Meta-analysis of Antecedents, Correlates, and Consequences." *Journal of Vocational Behavior* 61 (1): 20–52. doi:10.1006/jvbe.2001.1842.

Morgan, Robert M. and Shelby D. Hunt. 1994. "The Commitment - Trust Theory of Relationship Marketing." *Journal of Marketing* 58 (3): 20–38.

Nadadur, Ramanujam D. 2007. "Self-censorship in the Pakistani Print Media." *South Asian Survey* 14 (1): 45–63.

"Negative facets of news media." 2013. *Pakistan Media Commission Review*. Retrieved from http://mediacommissionreview.org/negative-facets-of-news-media/#.V3gNRzkrK8U.

Pintak, Lawrence, and Nazir J. Syed. 2013. "Pakistani Journalism: At the Crossroads of Muslim Identity, National Priorities and Journalistic Culture." *Media, Culture & Society* 35: 640–665. doi:10.1177/0163443713483654.

Pintak, Lawrence, and Nazir J. Syed. 2014. "Media, Policies, and Conflict in Pakistan." *Columbia Journalism Review*, April 25. http://www.cjr.org/behind_the_news/media_policy_and_conflict_in_p.php.

Pratt, Cornelius B., and Nadeem Akhtar. 2013. "Pakistan's Muffled, Fettered News Media and the (Questionable) Relevance of Western Journalistic Values to them." In *Edition International Media Studies: Vol. 5. Pakistańs Media Landscape: The Effects of Liberalization*, edited by Christoph Schmidt, 128–149. Berlin: VISTAS Verlag GmbH.

Ramaprasad, Jyotika. 2013. "Pakistan's Journalists: Profile, Epistemologies and Ethics." In *Edition International Media Studies: Vol. 5. Pakistańs Media Landscape: The Effects of Liberalization*, edited by Christoph Schmidt, 87–101. Berlin: VISTAS Verlag GmbH.

Reichheld, Frederick F. 2001. *Loyalty Rules! How Today's Leaders Build Lasting Relationships*. Boston: Harvard Business School Press.

Reporters without borders. 2016. "Targeted on all Sides." https://rsf.org/en/pakistan.

Ricchiardi, Sherry. 2012. *Challenges for Independent News Media in Pakistan*. Washington, DC: Center for International Media Assistance.

Rotter, Julian B. 1967. "A New Scale for the Measurement of Interpersonal Trust." *Journal of Personality*, 35: 651–665.

"Secret Funds Case: List of 282 Journalists Made Public." 2013. *Express Tribune*, April 22. tribune.com.pk/story/538900/secret-funds-case-list-of-282-journalists-to-be-made-public-today/.

Shah, Bina. 2015. "Journalism in Pakistan: Fear and Favor." *New York Times*, September 28. http://www.nytimes.com/2015/09/26/opinion/bina-shah-journalism-in-pakistan-fear-and-favor.html?_r=0.

Shimp, Terence A. 2010. *Advertising, Promotion, and other Aspects of Integrated Marketing Communications*,8th ed). Mason, OH: Thompson South-Western.

Strömbäck, Jesper, and Michael Karlsson. 2011. "Who's got the Power?" *Journalism Practice* 5 (6): 643–656.

Strömbäck, Jesper, Michael A. Mitrook, and Spiro Kiousis. 2010. "Bridging Two Schools of Thought: Applications of Public Relations Theory to Political Marketing." *Journal of Political Marketing* 9: 73–92.

Temporal, Paul, and M. Marton Trott. 2001. *Romancing the Customer: Maximizing Brand Value through Powerful Relationship Management*. Singapore: Wiley.

"Top 10 most Dangerous Places for Journalists." 2015. Retrieved from http://listsurge.com/top-10-most-dangerous-places-for-journalists/.

Yamin, Saira. 2015. "Pakistan National Security, Dilemmas and Transition to Democracy." *Journal of Asian Security and International Affairs* 2 (1): 1–26.

Welch, Mary. 2006. "Rethinking Relationship Management." *Journal of CommunicationManagement* 10: 138–155. doi:10.1108/13632540610664706.

Wilson, Laurie J. 1994. "Excellent Companies and Coalition-building among the Fortune 500: A Value- and Relationship-based Theory." *Public Relations Review* 20: 333–343.

# REARTICULATING *NEW YORK TIMES V. SULLIVAN* AS A SOCIAL DUTY TO JOURNALISTS

**Aimee Edmondson**

*During the frenzied run of presidential primaries in 2016, Republican nominee Donald Trump vowed to "open up" libel laws to make suing the media easier. This apparent attempt to resurrect seditious libel brought a flurry of debate about how American libel laws might be altered in this context. "We are going to have people sue you like you've never got sued before," Trump said. This article seeks to rearticulate the landmark* New York Times v. Sullivan *decision as a case about social duty and the duty that is owed to journalists in an increasingly contentious political climate. I argue that protecting this right to criticize public officials and public figures is as important as ever in our democratic system.* Sullivan *was a case about civil rights, about the right of African-American leaders and the media to cover and criticize how the police behaved in the 1960s when faced with the social revolution of the civil rights movement. This essay also focuses on three previously unstudied cases filed by police officers in the New York area in the 1960s.* Sullivan *secured our right to speak without a vindictive government bearing down on us via our legal system, but other cases decided outside the national spotlight suggest how that right was further cemented by the interaction of the media and the civil rights movement. Be it the brutality of police 50 years ago and today, or coverage of presidential candidates, I argue that journalists and the public are owed this right.*

## Introduction: The Duty to Criticize

What an uncanny *déjà vu*. Place the photographs side by side, images of protestors in Ferguson, Missouri, from 2014 and those of the civil rights demonstrations in the American South some 50 years earlier. "I am Mike Brown" placards might be the modern equivalent of the now famous "I Am A Man" signs from the 1968 Memphis sanitation workers' strike.[1] Michael Brown, an 18-year-old African American, was shot and killed by a white police officer on August 9, 2014, sparking widespread demonstrations and an international conversation about police militarization, tactics, and institutional racism. Other iconic images from the 1960s found their way back to mainstream media in the wake of the Ferguson controversy and in the aftermath of other high-profile cases of police officers shooting black males in cities across the United States. For example, Alabama lawman Bull Connor made an international spectacle out of Birmingham in 1963 with his lunging police dogs and skin-shredding fire hoses that washed young civil rights protesters down the street and into newspapers and television broadcasts around the world. All these years later, as coverage of white police officers shooting African-American men dominated the headlines month after month, the national conversation has swarmed around the issue of police brutality and has brought questions about how far we have come—or have not come—since the days of Bull. During the civil rights revolution of the 1950s and 1960s, such imagery swayed public opinion about America's black–white caste system and ushered in sweeping legal reforms in a wide range of areas. It is difficult to know what the more recent protests will mean for America's not so post-racial society. The handwritten signs of protesters around the country have roared, again and again since Ferguson:

> "Hands up, don't shoot."[2]
>
> "I can't breathe."[3]
>
> "Black Lives Matter."[4]

Though not as famous, other modern-day placards held by demonstrators have been bold in their criticism of police behavior in Ferguson and elsewhere:

> "KKK in Uniform, License to Kill, Please Stop!"
>
> "Police everywhere, justice nowhere."
>
> "The Whole Damn System is Racist as Hell."[5]

In light of this robust discourse, we must be careful not to take for granted our right to criticize police and individual government representatives acting in their official duties. Yet it is our responsibility as citizens to do so, according to the US Supreme Court's interpretation of the Constitution. In one of the most famous First Amendment cases in American history, *New York Times v. Sullivan*, Justice William Brennan wrote in 1964 that not only is it our right, it is our duty to criticize our government and its official representatives. This includes police officers, individuals employed by the state who have enormous power over the citizenry.

This essay seeks to rearticulate the landmark 52-year-old *Sullivan* case—and lawsuits similar to it—as a case about social duty and the duties owed to journalists in an increasingly contentious political climate. It argues that protecting this right to criticize public officials and public figures is as important as ever. The *Sullivan* case was in essence a case about speech relating to police brutality during the civil rights movement, as elected law enforcement officials took issue with a *New York Times* advertisement critical of their treatment of civil rights protesters in Alabama (Hall and Urofsky 2011). Brennan wrote eloquently of our "profound national commitment to the principle that debate on public issues should be uninhibited, robust, and wide-open, and that it may well include vehement, caustic and sometimes unpleasantly sharp attacks on government and public officials" (*New York Times v. Sullivan* 1964, 270). This issue is as critical now as it was then, though perhaps that fact has been forgotten by some. Consider statements by Republican presidential candidate Donald Trump, who in the frenzied run of presidential primaries in 2016 promised that if elected he would work to change libel laws in the United States so that he and other officials could successfully sue news organizations who write critically of them. "We're going to open up libel laws," Trump told the media at a rally in Texas in early 2016, "and we're going to have people sue you like you've never got sued before" (Gold 2016). Trump appeared to be taking aim at the *New York Times* and *Washington Post*, and despite his own attacks on political figures inside and outside his party, he has suggested a distaste for criticism of individual government representatives acting in their official duties: the very act that Justice Brennan wrote was so vital under the First Amendment. It is difficult to imagine any serious debate about changing the nation's libel laws, and such a move would arguably exceed a president's authority. However, Callum Borchers of the *Washington Post* outlined a concerning scenario:

> Alternatively, Trump could simply use the bully pulpit to promote a culture of frivolous libel suits that ultimately wouldn't go anywhere but would force media companies to spend precious resources on defending themselves. If his goal is to cause news outlets to lose money, Trump could conceivably achieve that objective without changing any laws at all. (Borchers 2016)

This fits the very description of the SLAPP (Strategic Lawsuits Against Public Participation) suits identified by Pring and Canan (1996), suits that discourage and punish those who speak out about issues of public concern. Trump might not feel defamed, this essay will argue, but he certainly suggests an interest in punishing those who speak or write critically of him.

Trump's statement and the resulting flurry of discussion on social media and in traditional news outlets provides an apt opportunity to reconsider journalists' First Amendment rights under pre-1964 libel laws: that is, pre-*Sullivan*. During the middle of the twentieth century, the media and civil rights protestors often faced financially crippling libel suits filed by public officials and even police officers, angered about criticism of their tactics or their brutality. A journalist's job is compromised if she or he is not free to cover a public official or political figure running for office. Trump may not know it, but *Sullivan* was a case about civil rights, about the right of African-American leaders and the media to cover and criticize how the Montgomery, Alabama, police force behaved in the 1960s when faced with the social revolution of the civil rights movement. *Sullivan* secured for journalists a right to carry out their work without a vindictive government bearing down on us via our legal system. In a time when politicians like Donald Trump are seeking to punish journalists for their political coverage, this essay examines more thoroughly the legal history of US libel law. Specifically, it offers context and analysis of three previously unstudied libel cases filed by police officers in the New York City area in 1964 and 1965 that further illustrate the fact that government representatives (police officers) were turning to libel to silence their critics even after the Supreme Court in *Sullivan* made it extremely difficult—if not impossible—for the police officers to win such cases.

## *Sullivan* and *Sullivan*-like Cases as Part of a Historic Pattern

The argument presented here offers consideration of the consequences of Trump's anti-news-media assault and demands for revision of libel laws by looking at the past uses of libel to punish the media and other government critics in the United States. Specifically, it considers the broader legal context surrounding *Sullivan* in an attempt to draw a connection to Trump's comments and what such an "opening up" of libel laws might mean in modern public discourse. A broader discussion of *Sullivan* and *Sullivan*-like cases is highly relevant—and should be at the forefront of national conversation—especially since 2014's Ferguson, Missouri, unrest. What could be more important to a democracy than covering the behavior of public officials, be it the brutality of police 50 years ago and today, or the speech of candidates for president of the United States?

In a post-*Sullivan* world, journalists who report fairly and accurately have little fear of retribution via libel law—and this is no small thing. Democracies must protect and encourage journalists and journalism and not attempt to resurrect seditious libel, per Trump's suggestion. This essay employs legal historical analysis of previously unstudied libel jurisprudence relating to demonstrations and speech criticizing the actions of police. It is because of those civil rights protests—including complaints of police brutality—in the 1950s and 1960s that we are able to criticize police brutality today, without fear of costly libel suits. In our system, press equals public, and indeed members of the public as well as journalists are owed this right.

Police brutality against the citizenry—what could be more worthy of public debate? This certainly was a major issue during the American civil rights movement, when a full-page advertisement placed in the *New York Times* in March 1960 criticized actions of police and public officials in southern cities, including Montgomery, Alabama. The advertisement, paid for by a civil rights group and entitled "Heed Their Rising Voices," spoke of the struggle in the South and police mistreatment of demonstrators as part of its plea for support for the growing movement (*New York Times* 1960, 25). Lester Bruce Sullivan, Montgomery's police commissioner, argued that the criticism of his police force was based on false statements and reflected negatively on him as the individual in charge of the police force. He filed a libel suit against the *New York Times* and others for the advertisement, one of many libel suits filed by police and public officials in the South for civil rights coverage. His was the first case to reach the US Supreme Court. Before this case, a libel plaintiff (the person bringing the suit) could recover damages if he or she could prove what was written or spoken was about him or her was false. Damages were presumed if the content was based on false information. Though he was not identified in the advertisement, Commissioner Sullivan argued successfully before the Alabama Supreme Court that this advertisement amounted to false and defamatory criticism of him, winning a record $500,000 verdict. The nation's high court overturned the decision, however, seeing Sullivan's suit as an attempt to resurrect seditious libel—that is, criticism of governing officials. The court agreed that the *New York Times* had been punished for criticizing the government, specifically the actions of government representatives in Montgomery, Alabama. This was the very thing, Justice Brennan said in *Sullivan* in 1964, that the First Amendment was supposed to guard against. This is the very thing that candidate Trump argued should be easier to punish.

Justice Hugo Black, an Alabama native, met the issue of race head on in his concurring opinion in *Sullivan*, arguing that libel law was being used to stop the civil rights movement in its tracks: "One of the acute and highly emotional issues in this country arises out of efforts of many people, even including some public officials, to continue state-commanded segregation of races in the public schools and other public places, despite our several holdings that such a state practice is forbidden by the Fourteenth Amendment" (*New York Times v. Sullivan* 1964, 294–295). *Sullivan* shifted the burden of proof in libel cases from the defendant to the plaintiff. This was a monumental shift. Now it is the burden of the plaintiff to prove that what was written or spoken about him was false, rather than the burden of the defendant to prove the information was true. The case also introduced the notion of "fault" in this context. Under this new actual malice standard of fault, the plaintiff has to show that the defendant published false information with a high degree of fault, that is, knowingly or recklessly. The US Supreme Court had not previously considered a libel case in the freedom-of-speech context. Libel laws were state laws, and the First Amendment did not protect libel or slander (Friedman 2002). The US Supreme Court's reversal of *Sullivan* marked not only a fundamental change in the law but set a course for First Amendment theory that in turn would help alter the course of the civil rights movement. The Supreme Court ruled that in order to win a suit, a public official like Sullivan must prove the *New York Times* knew the material was false or that it exhibited "reckless disregard for the truth" when it printed the information. Sullivan could not meet that tough new standard, it was found. Key in this decision: the First Amendment protects even false statements about public officials as long as they were made innocently. Justice Brennan in the *Sullivan* decision spoke of the "chilling effect"—if citizens were afraid that what they were saying could in some small way be factually incorrect, they would be afraid to speak at all. I argue that this would be the new world order a President Trump would seem likely to prefer.

Police Commissioner Sullivan was not alone in his effort to stop speech about the behavior of police officers. There is increasing evidence and argument that police officers used existing libel laws in the 1950s and early 1960s to craft what amounted to a sedition law in order to stop the press from covering the civil rights struggle and to stop civil rights leaders who criticized them (Edmondson 2011; Lewis 1991). It has been well established that had the US Supreme Court failed to overturn *Sullivan*, the case's impact on the civil rights movement would have been enormous (Lewis 1991; Smolla 1986). The *New York Times*—unarguably the leader in the mainstream media in its coverage of the emerging race beat down South prior to Sullivan's suit—was effectively shut out of the state of Alabama and forced to rely on wire reports of civil rights demonstrations until *Sullivan* was overturned. Without the world looking at the South through the lens of the national press, southern officials and other segregationists would have been free to continue to squelch activism in their own way.

## *"The Cup of Genocide": Other Cases in the South*

Libel suits from police arose out of the Birmingham bus station beatings during the 1961 Freedom Rides. Libel suits from police arose out of the University of Mississippi (Ole Miss) riots in 1962 as James Meredith sought to desegregate Mississippi's flagship university. They arose out of the 1963 March on Washington. They arose out of the Freedom Summer murders of three civil rights workers in Philadelphia, Mississippi, in 1964 (Edmondson 2011). Still more were filed for coverage of police shootings that were not attached to a particular civil rights-related event. These legal battles have not gotten the same attention as bombed churches, beaten and bloody Freedom Riders, or civil rights workers mysteriously disappearing in the night. But the cases remain an important piece of the civil rights story, as well as an insidious shackling of free-speech rights. In the instances discussed here, the plaintiffs were white police officers. The defendants were typically members of the media and civil rights leaders quoted in media outlets as criticizing police brutality. It is important to place these cases in context with modern criticism of police brutality, especially considering that a presidential candidate of a major political party suggested American libel law should return to the pre-1964 era.

Take, for example, Pulitzer Prize winner Hazel Brannon Smith's court battle in 1954 as an illustration that the northern media were not the only ones getting sued over the civil rights story. The editor of the *Lexington Advertiser* in Mississippi, Smith was sued by the local sheriff for an editorial she wrote about his harassment of black citizens. Smith opined that the sheriff should resign after he harassed a group of African-American men and accidentally shot one person in the leg (Kaul 2001). This case is remarkable in its similarity to *Sullivan*, where a local officer of the law turned to the court to take out his anger about criticism of his official duties. This suit was filed six years before *Sullivan*, illustrating that libel was an emerging weapon being used against those critical of police well before Sullivan's case (Edmondson 2014).

In March 1960, *Sullivan* and a host of companion cases were filed by Montgomery public officials against the *New York Times* and four civil rights leaders (*New York Times v. Sullivan* 1964). The governor of Alabama even added his name to the list of plaintiffs in this series of suits arguably designed to silence discourse relating to the civil rights movement. A month later, Birmingham, Alabama, leaders—most notably Police Commissioner Bull Connor—filed libel suits against the *New York Times* and one of its reporters for coverage there. These cases arose out of reporter Harrison Salisbury's stories that ran in April 1960, two weeks after the "Heed Their Rising Voices" advertisement appeared. Salisbury, a Pulitzer Prize winner and a former *New York Times* Moscow correspondent, wrote a front-page story headlined "Fear and Hatred Grip Birmingham" and infuriated Birmingham's establishment (McWhorter 2001; Nunnelley 1991). Connor and other Birmingham officials sought damages for Salisbury's story on racial tensions that said "every inch of middle ground has been fragmented by the emotional dynamite of racism, reinforced by the whip, the razor, the gun, the bomb, the torch, the club, the knife, the mob, the police and many branches of the state's apparatus" (Salisbury 1960). What is sometimes missing from legal scholars' writings about these cases is their context within the civil rights movement. For example, plaintiffs Sullivan and Connor were the police officers who also gave mobs of Ku Klux Klansmen time to waylay Freedom Riders at the Montgomery and Birmingham bus stations before calling in their officers to haul the wounded demonstrators off to jail in 1961 (Smith 1996). Connor and other city officials sued CBS for reporter Howard K. Smith's 1961 documentary on the Freedom Riders' bus station beatings, "Who Speaks for Birmingham?" Those beatings, captured on film by a *Birmingham News* photographer, threw a blinding spotlight on the city. Prompted by Salisbury's reporting, Smith had gone to Birmingham to see if the *New York Times* reporter was exaggerating the conditions in the South and said he found it even worse than expected, noting that police appeared to be in cahoots with the Klan.

It is important to note the historical pattern of police officers' efforts to silence all critics and agitators, not just in the deep South and not just against the mainstream media. For example, leaders of the National Association for the Advancement of Colored People (NAACP) and *The Black Dispatch* were sued for libel by a police officer in Oklahoma City, Oklahoma, after civil rights activists and black journalists reported on the killing of a youngster, Albert E. Scott, in that city. This was in 1960, the same year as the *Sullivan* suit, and also situated in the context of civil rights discourse. The suit was filed after the newspaper published a letter from NAACP leaders that characterized the incident as a lynching on the part of police (*Pierce v. Moon* 1960). These suits could be financially devastating to local organizations and smaller media outlets. I argue that this issue has important implications today, for any individual, be it a civil rights activist in Ferguson, Missouri, or a journalist covering a story. I also argue that such devastation is Trump's goal in "opening up" libel laws, punishing media companies for being critical of him, the very definition of SLAPP suits as identified by Pring and Canan (1996).

The Ole Miss riot in the fall of 1962 brought with it a flurry of libel litigation, most notably from conservative personality and retired army general Edwin A. Walker. *Associated Press v. Walker* (1967) extended *Sullivan*'s actual malice requirement to public figures, rather than just public officials, thus continuing the Supreme Court's rewriting of libel law through civil rights-related suits. Walker filed scores of suits against the individual newspapers that ran an Associated Press story reporting that he helped lead the charge against federal marshals working to keep the peace as James Meredith desegregated the campus by court order. Among Walker's many suits was a case against venerable *Atlanta Constitution* editor Ralph McGill, for a syndicated column about Walker's involvement in the riots. Hodding Carter Jr. of the Greenville *Delta Democrat-Times* also faced Walker in a slander case based on remarks the noted publisher made about him at the University of New Hampshire's Distinguished Lecture Series (*Walker v. Carter* 1962). Walker was a former US military leader who kept law and order in Little Rock, Arkansas, when Central High School was desegregated in the 1957. He later said he was on the wrong side of the battle and should have refused President Eisenhower's decision to deploy federal troops to maintain law and order in the South. Journalists McGill and Carter won Pulitzer Prizes for their editorials in favor of civil rights legislation and desegregation, and as such, were huge targets for racists like Walker, also a former candidate for the governor of Texas.

The Ole Miss riots also brought a suit from Mississippi Highway Patrol Commander T. B. Birdsong, who hated the way the national media portrayed his troopers. Stinging from the coverage in the days following the riot, Birdsong was particularly irked by a story in the *Saturday Evening Post* called "What Next in Mississippi?" by Robert Massie, a freelancer living in New York who witnessed the Ole Miss riots in Oxford on September 30, 1962. Like the scores of other reporters on the scene, Massie portrayed the white protestors as the armed aggressors and the federal marshals sent there to keep order as overwhelmed (Massie 1962). Governor Ross Barnett had whipped the protestors into a frenzy, appearing on statewide television and declaring on the radio that Mississippi was a sovereign state that would not obey the court's desegregation orders. Racial mixing, according to Barnett, was unthinkable and would lead to the demise of the pure white race. He famously roared about his resistance to a court order to admit Meredith: "NEVER! ... We will not drink from the cup of genocide" (Dittmer 1991).

Birdsong filed a $220 million libel suit for Massie's article, which said his men failed to help federal marshals rein in the mob that night (*Curtis Publishing v. Birdsong* 1966). Birdsong said he and his men were libeled in these two sentences about the riots that killed two people and wounded more than 100 others: "A sizable portion of the blame must go to the gray-uniformed men of the Mississippi Highway Patrol. 'Those bastards just walked off and left us,' said one top official of the Department of Justice" (Massie 1962). Birdsong took exception to "those bastards," which he said were "obscene and fighting words" that reflected on his personal reputation and that of his officers (*Curtis Publishing v. Birdsong* 1966). Stories like Massie's for the *Saturday Evening Post* overwhelmingly painted the Mississippi officers in a bad light. Massie, for example, wrote that a state patrolman laughed as white protesters slashed the tires of an army truck. He also said a state trooper stood by while a mob beat up a news photographer. "An Oxford woman rushed over to the state trooper. 'Aren't you going to stop them?' she cried. The patrolman grinned at her. 'I don't see nothin', lady, do you?'" (Massie 1962).

Well after the US Supreme Court overturned *Sullivan*, Curtis Publishing (which owned the *Saturday Evening Post*) argued before the Fifth Circuit that the actual-malice doctrine applied because the alleged libel concerned criticism of public officials in the performance of their official duties. The appeals court reversed the lower court's decision. But it did not even reference the *Sullivan* ruling, by then more than a year old. There was no discussion about the need to prove actual malice when writing about a public official. Instead, the appeals court focused on jurisdictional problems and the use of the words "those bastards." The Fifth Circuit agreed with Curtis Publishing that the word "bastard" did not defame Birdsong: "It is not entirely clear whether the plaintiffs are alleging that by the use of the phrase 'those bastards' the allegedly libelous article questioned the legitimacy of their birth" (*Curtis Publishing v. Birdsong* 1966). The court said no reasonable person would believe that the reporter accused every patrolman on duty at Ole Miss "of having been born out of wedlock." The court said that the words "reflect more on the character of the user" than on the person to whom they are referring. The media won this case, but it took years and untold amounts of money in legal fees to secure their First Amendment right to criticize police actions in the wake of the civil rights movement.

Another case remarkably *Sullivan*-like was filed by an Alabama sheriff against *Ladies Home Journal* over a story about the March on Washington in August 1963. Etowah County Sheriff Dewey Colvard said Curtis Publishing libeled him in the article, "Sophronia's Grandson Goes to Washington," written by the playwright Lillian Hellman (1963). Part of her story included a flashback to Gadsden, Alabama, where she wrote that local police shocked demonstrators with electric cattle prods to disperse the crowds (*New York Times* 1964).

### *"Wanted for Murder": Protesting Police Brutality*

A trio of cases from the New York City area in 1964 and 1965 further highlights the fact that police officers were turning to libel to silence their critics even after *Sullivan* made it extremely difficult for the police to win them. These three cases also illustrate that it was not just southern lawmen seeking to silence criticism of their official actions.[6] On July 16, 1964, off-duty New York City Police Lt. Thomas Gilligan shot and killed James Powell, a 15-year-old African American. The incident brought protests in Harlem that spread to the Bedford-Stuyvesant area of New York during a three-day riot in which more than 200 stores were damaged and 122 people arrested. Lt. Gilligan, dressed in civilian clothes, said he heard a commotion on the street and saw a man with a knife in his hand pursing another person. He said he identified himself as a police lieutenant, flashing his badge and revolver, but that the young man, Powell, came toward him with his knife. Lt. Gilligan said he advised the man to stop and fired a warning shot. He then fired at Powell in self-defense, killing him instantly (*Gilligan v. King* 1965). In sum, Gilligan fired three shots and "was still standing there when girls on the street became hysterical. One kept screaming, 'Go ahead, kill another nigger'" (Davis 1965). A crowd of 300 formed suddenly and began stoning police who had arrived, and the full-scale riot then followed. The Harlem Defense Council published a poster reading, "Wanted for Murder." It included a photo of Gilligan in his police uniform and identified him as "Gilligan, the cop." Newspaper, television, and radio reporters said that Gilligan weighed about 200 pounds and was six feet tall and that Powell was only 15 and had a slight build. Protestors used that poster in their marches and attached them to buildings and power poles in the city.

Gilligan was exonerated by a grand jury and internal police department investigations, which held that he killed in self-defense after being attacked with a knife. He then filed a $5.25 million libel suit alleging he had been falsely accused of murder by numerous civil rights leaders, including James Farmer and Martin Luther King Jr. Gilligan argued that he was not an elected official, as Sullivan was in his position as a police commissioner. He argued that he was one of thousands of low-ranking government employees who are not public officials and that therefore he would not have to prove "actual malice," that higher standard of fault where the plaintiff must prove that the defendant communicated the allegedly libelous information "with knowledge of falsity or reckless disregard for the truth" (*Gilligan v. Farmer* 1965).

The defendants argued that police should have to prove "actual malice" rather than the much easier "negligence" standard of fault. They argued that the *Sullivan* opinion was designed to help foster robust debate on public issues and to bring about "political and social changes desired by the people" (*Gilligan v. Farmer* 1965, 215). Farmer and King's attorneys argued that in a literal sense, anyone who occupied a position in government, even a minor position, is a public official. "It is not the title of his office but the duties … which the particular officer" has that matters (*Gilligan v. Farmer* 1965, 216). And indeed, police officers—more than most any other government officials—have astounding power over the citizenry. Ultimately the Supreme Court of New York agreed with the civil rights leaders in this case, that Gilligan—like Sullivan—must prove actual malice. This case, then, definitively extended the actual malice requirement to police officers, yet it has not been studied extensively by legal scholars. Almost a year to the day later, another police shooting brought publicity about police brutality and yet another libel suit. An African-American man known by his neighbors to be mentally ill was shadow boxing on the sidewalk in his Brooklyn neighborhood of Bedford-Stuyvesant on a hot and steamy day in July 1965. He often prayed and talked to himself, but otherwise seemed harmless. New to the beat on this particular day was Sheldon Leibowitz, a white 28-year-old rookie patrolman, who spotted the man, Nelson Erby, behaving strangely. Witnesses' reports differ on what happened next. Some said Erby had dropped to his knees to pray for rain, for relief from the heat, as he had done many times before. Patrolman Leibowitz ordered him to stop, but Erby did not "move along" so instructed. The official police report said Erby hit out at the police officer, the two struggled, and then Erby pulled out a knife with a five-inch blade. Police said Leibowitz was handcuffing Erby to arrest him for disturbing the peace when Erby lunged at him, and then in the ensuing struggle, the officer was hit in the left forearm by a bullet from his own pistol. A passing truck driver, Stewart Maxwell, 20, told police that Erby had the gun and that Maxwell hit him with a nightstick he kept in his truck. Leibowitz was able to get his gun back and shoot Erby after the man ignored his warning to stand back. Erby died at the scene (*Newsday* 1965a; Lieberman and Seely 1965).

The local chapter of the Congress for Racial Equality (CORE) said the shooting happened much differently. Members of CORE said Erby "was mentally defective" and "like a child," and that the police should have treated him as such (*Newsday* 1965b). Instead, Erby was shot in cold blood by a rookie cop who did not know the neighborhood or Erby. CORE brought forth witnesses who said Erby never had possession of the patrolman's gun and that there had been no knife. The organization held a protest at the intersection where the shooting occurred and organized a protest march over the bridge from Brooklyn, a total of eight miles, to police headquarters in Manhattan. Some 150 demonstrators carried signs protesting police brutality and demanded a civilian review board to independently consider evidence in such cases, along with fielding community complaints about police. CORE members also were quoted heavily in several newspapers throughout the city in the following days. CORE's James Farmer sent a telegram to Police Commissioner Vincent Broderick saying the shooting indicated the possibility of "police culpability," and this telegram was widely covered and quoted by the media. After an all-white grand jury declined to indict Leibowitz on criminal charges, CORE leaders said civil rights leaders were "seriously disturbed" by the patrolman's exoneration. A statement, also widely quoted in local newspapers, read: "We again emphasize that this case, as countless cases in the past, dramatizes the vastly inadequate system of police review adjudication in New York City" (*Newsday* 1965b)

Leibowitz filed a libel suit in October 1965 against CORE, naming several members personally, along with other civil rights groups who had engaged in public dialogue about the shooting specifically and police brutality generally. Leibowitz said the civil rights leaders "conspired and maliciously and wilfully participated in a plan and course of action designed to defame and injure the plaintiff in his good name and reputation in his profession as a policeman, to destroy his income and livelihood, and to remove plaintiff as a police officer" in New York City. At the crux of his complaint was a poster or handbill that read: "Wanted for Murder" and included a picture of him in his police uniform, his name and precinct. It was signed by the Harlem Defense Council. Seeking $2.5 million in damages, Liebowitz's attorney used the language of the *Sullivan* decision months earlier, asserting that the poster was published with actual malice, with reason to believe it false and with the intent of exposing him to "hatred, contempt, ridicule and aversion and injure and dishonor him" as a police officer (*Liebowitz* v. *Farmer* 1965). He even sued the printer who made the poster. The NAACP mounted a hearty defense, filing motion after motion and pointing to the March 1964 *Sullivan* case and Justice Brennan's clearly stated opinion about a citizen's right and duty to criticize police actions. At the end of 1966, New York County judge Abraham Geller dismissed the suit.

In a third case in the New York City area, another police officer shot and killed an African-American man in 1965. Civil rights leaders criticized him for murder and were slapped with a libel suit. Henry Martinez was a patrolman in Newark, New Jersey; police said Martinez shot Lester Long in the head after a routine traffic stop and that Long was stopped because of a noisy muffler and a defective headlight on his car. The initial report released by police said Martinez' gun went off accidentally when he tripped on a curb. The story was later changed, and police reported that Martinez shot him because Long had a knife and had slashed at the officer's partner, William Provost. As Long fled, Martinez reportedly drew his gun and ordered him to halt. Long kept running, so Martinez aimed and fired, killing him in the street (*Martinez v. CORE* 1965).

Leaders of CORE demanded that Martinez be suspended, and created handwritten signs that they mimeographed and distributed that read: "Stop Police Brutality. Our neighbor, Lester Long, Jr., was murdered by a policeman last Friday night on the corner of Oriental and Broadway, shot in the back of the head." The flyers urged people to join CORE at a rally and protest on June 16 at 7 pm at the street corner where Long was shot. City leaders suspended the officer while the investigation was pending in June 1965. The mayor said he ordered Martinez's suspension to prevent racial disorder; nearly half of Newark's 400,000 residents were African American. Martinez was reinstated after the Newark Human Rights Commission said its investigation indicated there was no evidence of racial prejudice in the case and before an Essex County grand jury had determined he was legally justified in the amount of force used (*Martinez v. CORE* 1965).

Martinez complained in his libel suit that "he was deprived of his position as a patrolman, his reputation has been and will be injured due to the great deal of publicity attached to his illegal suspension, he has suffered and will suffer mental anguish requiring medical attention, and he and his family have suffered special damages and his position in the community has been seriously damaged." Farmer, CORE's national director, was handed court documents accusing him of libel conspiracy shortly before he spoke at a civil rights rally organized by CORE in Military Park. Under heavy police guard because of death threats, Farmer addressed a crowd of about 700, demanding the creation of a civilian police review board (*Ocala Star-Banner* 1965). Farmer distributed a flyer that read in part, "Henry Martinez is a murderer," and for that, he and 11 others were sued for libel. After more than a year of legal maneuvering, NAACP lawyers succeeded in getting the suit dismissed. While the defendants ultimately prevailed, it is important to note that they were forced to come up with hefty lawyers' fees in order to defend their right to speak. The same NAACP lawyers were fighting legal battles on a wide variety of fronts to secure basic civil rights for African Americans. The libel suits pulled them away from such cases and into civil court, case after case, year after year.

*The Afro American* (1965) offered context to the CORE libel case, pointing out that similar suits had been filed by police officers accused of brutality in six states. It was rare for news articles to provide such context for these libel suits, but that context is one of the most important contributions legal historical scholars can provide when similar concerns are raised in today's political and social-legal environment. Outside of the spotlight that nation-altering cases such as *Sullivan* produce, dozens of cases in the area of libel have gone unexplored; the layers at the intersection of race, law, and journalism are much deeper and more complex than historians and legal scholars generally assume. In a broader sense, this research might remind us that major social change rarely takes place as a result of one incident, but rather is the result of many actors and actions whose significance accumulates over time. This point is true of many social and political movements, and it further challenges our academic tendency to write about law and history as a parade of Great Men and Great Moments. Or in this instance, Great Court Cases, as *Sullivan* is surely one that any introductory media law or history textbook expounds upon with great detail.

## Discussion and Conclusion: The Protection of Civil and Journalistic Duties

Through the prism of libel law, it can be argued that the civil rights fight and its amplification in media coverage began much earlier and spread much more broadly than most research acknowledges. The media tried to inform the citizenry, to serve its watchdog function, to provide a venue for public discussion and debate. In some locales, it was not truly free to do so until many years after *Sullivan*. In addition, civil rights leaders faced intimidating and costly libel actions for many years, as the battles continued in the streets and in the courtroom. Police officers and their attorneys came to understand that criticism of their actions as law enforcement is protected by the First Amendment. This is why we can march today, to petition our government for redress of grievances, and most certainly report in the press, without fear of retribution via costly and intimidating libel suits. The posters stemming from the 2014 Ferguson shooting: "Wanted, Officer Darren Wilson, for the Murder of Mike Brown," is eerily similar to the posters that identified Officer Gilligan, Officer Leibowitz and Officer Martinez in 1965. Whatever its impact on public opinion, or on the life or career of a public employee, this criticism can thrive today because of those unheralded decisions of five decades ago.

Outside the context of criticism of police brutality, Pring and Canan (1996) identified a body of case law they dubbed "intimidation lawsuits": the SLAPP suits discussed above. In these suits, plaintiffs arguably do not feel defamed, but rather seek to silence critics. Such cases have become a growing legal threat for anyone speaking about issues of public concern. Most of these fail in court, but Pring and Canan estimated that between 1976 and 1996, thousands of people were sued into silence. Corporations have used SLAPP suits as a deterrent against nonprofit and citizen criticism in a wide range of areas. Most commonly, researchers found a pattern of real estate developers' cases against those protesting development for environmental reasons, for example.

Trump's call to alter libel laws could encourage public officials (or would-be public officials) to reinvigorate the notion of seditious libel. In early 2016 in Fort Worth, Texas, Trump proceeded with his customary rant against newspapers, especially the *New York Times* and the *Washington Post*, complaining that they are "losing money" and are "dishonest":

> One of the things I'm going to do if I win, and I hope we do and we're certainly leading. I'm going to open up our libel laws so when they write purposely negative and horrible and false articles, we can sue them and win lots of money. We're going to open up those libel laws. So when The New York Times writes a hit piece which is a total disgrace or when The Washington Post, which is there for other reasons, writes a hit piece, we can sue them and win money instead of having no chance of winning because they're totally protected. (Volokh 2016)

To clarify, journalists are not "totally protected" from libel suits. Provable truth is the ultimate defense in a libel suit, and if reporters get it wrong, there are ramifications. If they get it wrong and the plaintiff is a public official or public figure, as Trump certainly is, they may still lose a libel case if actual malice is proven. The 1964 Republican presidential candidate, Senator Barry Goldwater, prevailed in his libel suit against *Fact* magazine over "The Unconscious of a Conservative: A Special Issue on the Mind of Barry Goldwater," which had appeared shortly before the election (Miller 2006). The magazine contended that Goldwater had a severely paranoid personality and was psychologically unfit to be president. Under the *Sullivan* standard, the defendants were found to have acted with actual malice: knowledge that the material was false or with reckless disregard of whether the information was false. The US Supreme Court refused to hear an appeal (Ginzburg v. Goldwater 1970).

Journalists are not, then, owed a blanket immunity for reckless practice. But journalists, and by extension society, are owed the right to report and discuss the actions of those running for and holding elected office. Government certainly has a role in protecting journalists and journalism from frivolous and costly libel suits. But the issue reaches beyond fear of legal action. If civil rights leaders and those criticizing the actions of police or public officials fear costly libel suits, they might also be afraid to take to the streets or speak to journalists on such vital issues as police brutality. It is also important to point out that the *Sullivan* court made certain that the law does not require a statement to be perfectly accurate to be considered true. Some accidentally false statements must be protected in order to insure a robust public debate under the "substantial truth" doctrine. As long as the gist of the statement is correct, a defendant is likely to be protected. For example, Martin Luther King Jr. was arrested four times, not seven, according to the *New York Times* advertisement that sparked the *Sullivan* case in 1960. The protesting students in Montgomery sang "The Star Spangled Banner," not "My Country Tis of Thee," as reported in the advertisement. This raises another question: Might a media company use the substantial truth doctrine in a countersuit to justify collection of damages against a plaintiff who sued based on improper accusation of fault? It is a question worthy of consideration given Trump's statements relating to libel law.

The uneasy relationship between public officials and the government is as old as the nation itself. President George Washington railed about Philip Freneau of the *National Gazette*, who supported Thomas Jefferson's ideology and criticized the president's foreign policy. The president famously called the editor "that rascal Freneau," while Jefferson praised him for having "saved our Constitution which was galloping fast into monarchy" (Fellow 2005, 74). Fast forward to 1970 and we have vice president Spiro T. Agnew's angry rant against the press for covering his tax evasion charges, among other things, which would force his resignation and replacement by Gerald Ford. The words "nattering nabobs of negativism," Agnew's description of the press, were penned by William Safire and have found a home in the American consciousness. Then there is President George W. Bush's reference to the editor of the *New York Times* as "a major league asshole," a remark caught on a microphone which the president apparently did not realize was hot (Martinez 2015).

Words are one thing, but the legal actions of a vengeful government official against the press are entirely different. Trump calls the media "dishonest scum" for writing articles about him and his platform, though an all-out assault on the First Amendment is likely just bluster, writes Mathew Ingram (2016): "Even before he became a Republican presidential candidate, Donald Trump frequently made factually questionable pronouncements and stretched the bounds of credulity. And the real estate tycoon's recent announcement of how he planned to 'open up' U.S. libel laws if elected arguably also falls into this category."[7] Even if a candidate—or a president—should forget or ignore the duty of providing journalists with the breathing space to do their work, or to amplify the voices of civil rights leaders doing theirs, a broad set of decisions is in place to ensure that these essential civic and journalistic duties are protected.

## ACKNOWLEDGEMENTS

I would like to thank Fred Vultee and the anonymous referees for their feedback on this article. Views, errors, and omissions remain my own.

## DISCLOSURE STATEMENT

No potential conflict of interest was reported by the author.

## NOTES

1. "I am Michael Brown" or "I am Mike Brown" has been emblazoned on protestors' signs and worn on sweatshirts during protests in Ferguson, Missouri, and other American cities. Similarities were noted in the media at the time. See, for example, Kennedy and Schuessler (2014 ) and Bowerman (2014 ).

2. Witnesses reported that Brown was surrendering with his hands in the air when Ferguson police officer Darren Wilson shot and killed him. Other reports indicate that this was not true.
3. This slogan comes from the death of Eric Garner, who died July 17, 2014, when a New York police officer placed him in a chokehold during an arrest that was captured on video. The scuffle occurred when police attempted to arrest him for selling cigarettes illegally. A grand jury declined to indict the policeman in the death. Garner's family settled with the city over his death, ruled a homicide due to compression of the neck, for $5.9 million.
4. Across the country, demonstrators staged die-ins protesting Brown's and Garner's deaths. Other deaths prompting mass demonstrations include those of Tamir Rice, an unarmed 12-year-old in Cleveland in November 2014, and Freddie Gray, who died after suffering a spinal cord injury while in police custody in Baltimore in April 2014.
5. A basic Google images search using key words such as "Ferguson" and "protests" yielded a rich sample of messages on protesters' signs.
6. These three cases have not been addressed in secondary legal historical literature and are part of the author's larger study on the intersection of race, libel, and journalism. The cases were discovered in the archives of the NAACP legal files. In an effort to locate the universe of cases relevant to the study of race and libel, the author searched LexisNexis, HeinOnline, and Westlaw, using a variety of keyword combinations. However, many cases that would be relevant have not been reported in any legal journals because they only reached the trial level. Because they did not go to an appeals court, they would not appear in a law reporter and are not part an electronic reporting system, and therefore are not keyword searchable. Some cases included here also were located using a keyword search of the *New York Times* archive from 1955 to 1970. Editors and reporters at the *New York Times* were particularly attuned to the use of libel during the civil rights movement since this newspaper faced so many suits. Some cases also were identified through citations and footnotes in other libel cases. Still others were located through local newspaper coverage of the court proceedings in small towns like Gadsden, Alabama. Still more cases were located in more general works on the history of the movement where they were given only brief mention. An extensive search of civil rights histories and biographies of civil rights leaders and journalists who covered the movement yielded a paragraph or two here and there on previously obscure libel cases. This is by no means, then, the universe of cases, but rather a sampling to illustrate that *Sullivan* was not the only suit filed for charges relating to police brutality. This is in effect a series of case studies that may help civil rights scholars better understand the myriad battles ongoing in the courts: yet another way to understand the challenges of those who were combating the racist status quo.
7. Ingram notes that there is no federal libel law for Trump to "open up" or alter. Under the American system of government and American law, the Constitution does not specifically enumerate how the executive branch might expand libel law interpretation in light of the First Amendment protections afforded to speech and the press. Ingram points out that the president would have to convince all states to change the way they prosecute libel—which would go against *Sullivan*'s actual malice standard—or he would need to convince Congress to pass a federal law specifically governing libel. All states have their own libel laws, and those must adhere to the *Sullivan* actual malice standard put forth by the US Supreme Court in 1964.

## REFERENCES

*The Afro American*. 1965. "Jim Farmer Sued," July 31.

*Associated Press v. Walker*. 1967. 388 U.S. 130.

Borchers, Callum. 2016. "Donald Trump vowed to 'Open Up' Libel Laws to make suing the Media Easier. Can he do that?" *Washington Post*, February 26. https://www.washingtonpost.com/news/the-fix/wp/2016/02/26/donald-trump-vows-to-open-up-libel-laws-to-make-suing-the-media-easier-heres-how-he-could-do-it/.

Bowerman, Mary. 2014. "'I Am A Man' to "I Am Michael Brown': A Closer Look at Protest Slogans," *USA Today*, December 9.

*Curtis Publishing v. Birdsong*. 1966. 360 F.2d 344.

Davis, Alvin. 1965. "The New Tinderbox." *New York Post*, July 16.

Dittmer, John. 1991. *Local People, The Struggle for Civil Rights in Mississippi*. Chicago: University of Illinois Press.

Edmondson, Aimee. 2011. "In Sullivan's Shadow: The Use and Abuse of Libel Law Arising from the Civil Rights Movement, 1960–1989." *Journalism History* 37 (1): 27–38.

Edmondson, Aimee. 2014. "A Pulitzer from the North, A Libel Suit from the South: Reaction to Four Southern editors' Civil Rights Coverage, 1954–1967." *First Amendment Law Review* 12: 461–495.

Fellow, Anthony R. 2005. *American Media History*. Boston: Wadsworth, Cengage Learning.

Friedman, Lawrence M. 2002. *American Law in the Twentieth Century*. New Haven: Yale University Press.

*Gilligan v. Farmer*. 1965. Supreme Court of New York, 30 A.D.2d 26.

*Gilligan v. King*. 1965. 48 Msc.2d 212.

Ginzburg v. Goldwater. 1970. 397 U.S. 978.

Gold, Hadas. 2016. "Donald Trump: "We're going to 'Open Up' Libel Laws." *Politico*, February 26. http://www.politico.com/blogs/on-media/2016/02/donald-trump-libel-laws-219866.

Hall, Kermit L., and Melvin I. Urofsky. 2011. *New York Times v. Sullivan: Civil Rights, Libel Law, and the Free Press*. Lawrence: University Press of Kansas.

Hellman, Lillian. 1963. "Sophronia's Grandson Goes to Washington." *Ladies Home Journal* 80 (10): 78–81.

Ingram, Mathew. 2016. "Could Donald Trump Actually Make Good on His Promise to 'Open Up' Libel Laws?" *Fortune*, February 29. http://fortune.com/2016/02/29/trump-libel-law/.

Kaul, Arthur J. 2001. "Hazel Brannon Smith and the Lexington Advertiser." In *The Press and Race: Mississippi Journalists Confront the Movement*, edited by David R. Davies, 233–262. Jackson: University Press of Mississippi.

Kennedy, Randy, and Schuessler Jennifer. 2014. "Ferguson Images Evoke Civil Rights Era and Changing Visual Perceptions," *New York Times*, August 14.

Lewis, Anthony. 1991. *Make No Law, The Sullivan Case and the First Amendment*. New York: Random House.

Lieberman, Irving, and Nancy Seely. 1965. "Koota Starts Probe Into Killing by Cop." *New York Post*, July 16.

*Liebowitz v. Farmer*. 1965. County of New York, filed November 11.

Martinez, Jack. 2015. "Inside the GOP's War Against the Media." *Newsweek*, November 9. http://www.newsweek.com/republican-debates-media-bias-campaign-issue-392286.

*Martinez v. CORE*. 1965. Essex County Court, Law Division.

Massie, Robert. 1962. "What Next in Mississippi?" *Saturday Evening Post* 235 (18): 18–23.

McWhorter, Diane. 2001. *Carry Me Home*. New York: Simon and Schuster.

Miller, Stephen. 2006. "Ralph Ginzburg, 76, Magazine Publisher Who Tangled With Goldwater and Supreme Court." *The New York Sun*, July 7. http://www.nysun.com/obituaries/ralph-ginzburg-76-magazine-publisher-who-tangled/35617/.

*Newsday*. 1965a. "City Cop Kills a Negro; '64 Riot Scene Stays Quiet." July 16.

*Newsday*. 1965b. "Probe Clears Cop Who Shot Negro in City." July 23.

*New York Times*. 1960. "Heed Their Rising Voices." March 29. http://www.archives.gov/exhibits/documented-rights/exhibit/section4/detail/heed-rising-voices.html.

*New York Times*. 1964. "Curtis Publishing Is Named In a $3 Million Libel Suit." February 27. http://www.nytimes.com/1964/02/27/curtis-publishing-is-named-in-a-3-million-libel-suit.html.

*New York Times v. Sullivan*. 1964. 376 U.S. 254.

Nunnelley, William A. 1991. *Bull Connor*. Tuscaloosa: The University of Alabama Press.

*Ocala Star-Banner*. 1965. "Warrant Served On Farmer, Accused Of Libel Conspiracy." July 22.

*Pierce v. Moon*. 1960. Case No. 150,825, Oklahoma County, Oklahoma.

Pring, George W., and Penelope Canan. 1996. *SLAPPs, Getting Sued for Speaking Out*. Philadelphia: Temple University Press.

Salisbury, Harrison. 1960. "Fear and Hatred Grip Birmingham." *New York Times*, April 8. http://timesmachine.nytimes.com/timesmachine/1960/04/12/105426614.html?pageNumber=1.

Smith, Howard K. 1996. *Events Leading Up to My Death, The Life of a Twentieth-Century Reporter*. New York: St. Martin's Press.

Smolla, Rodney A. 1986. *Suing the Press*. New York: Oxford University Press.

Volokh, Eugene. 2016. "Donald Trump says he'll 'Open Up Libel Laws'." *The Washington Post*, February 26. https://www.washingtonpost.com/news/volokh-conspiracy/wp/2016/02/26/donald-trump-says-hell-open-up-libel-laws/.

*Walker v. Carter*. 1962. Cause No. 6182, Circuit Court of Washington County, Mississippi.

# WATCHING OVER THE WATCHDOGS
## The problems that Filipino journalists face

**Edson C. Tandoc Jr.**

*Studying the problems that journalists face is important, considering the role that journalists play in reporting about and legitimizing the problems that confront society. This study explores what journalists in the Philippines, a young democracy with a unique media ecology, consider to be the most important problem they face. Drawing on a survey of 349 Filipino journalists, this study found that journalists in the Philippines are most concerned about low pay, media violence, information access, and professionalism. Younger journalists tend to identify low pay as the most important problem, while the problem of violence against journalists was more salient for reporters than for editors and managers.*

### Introduction

The Philippine press is best described as a contradiction (Tandoc and Skoric 2010). It takes pride in being free from state control, unlike most press systems in its neighbors in Asia (Aguilar, Mendoza, and Candelaria 2014). And yet it is consistently ranked as among the most dangerous countries for journalists (Rosales 2006). The International Federation of Journalists (IFJ 2016) reported that 146 Filipino journalists had been murdered since 1990—the second highest number in the world, next only to Iraq. The Maguindanao Massacre, considered the deadliest single attack on journalists anywhere in the world, occurred in the southern Philippines during peacetime: 32 local journalists, covering the convoy of a political candidate, were shot dead in November 2009, their bodies buried in the mountain using government backhoes (Rauhala 2014). So far, none of the alleged masterminds—members of a powerful political clan—have been convicted (Rauhala 2014).

Numerous problems confront journalists around the world, especially during this period when the field of journalism is undergoing transformation (Tandoc 2014). Understanding these problems is important, considering the crucial role that journalists play in democratic societies, such as in the Philippines (Singer 1997). The problems that journalists face affect how they do their work, such as how they interact with public relations sources (Yun and Yoon 2011). However, literature on social problems has mostly focused on how social problems are represented and reported by journalists (Hilgartner and Bosk 1988; Schneider 1985). It is equally important to focus on the social problems confronting journalists. While journalists play an important role in defining, legitimizing, and addressing problems that affect society (Kitsuse and Spector 1973; Schneider 1985), the journalistic community also faces its own problems. This is particularly true in young democracies, such as the Philippines, where so much is expected of the press, but where structural support for journalists remains unstable (Aguilar, Mendoza, and Candelaria 2014; Gonzalez 1988; Rosales 2006; Shafer and Aregood 2012). Therefore, this study focuses on the problems encountered by journalists in the Philippines, a developing country in Asia also characterized by a unique media context. Based on a survey of Filipino journalists, this study explores what problems journalists define as most important, and what individual and organizational factors affect such perceptions.

## Literature Review

### *Defining Problems*

Sociologists have defined what constitutes a social problem in a number of ways. For example, Merton and Nisbet (1976, 7) argued that "a social problem exists when there is a sizeable discrepancy between what is and what people think ought to be." Fuller and Myers (1941, 320), on the other hand, argued that a "social problem is a condition which is defined by a considerable number of persons as a deviation from some social norm which they cherish." This definition is not only about an objective discrepancy between expectations and conditions, but also about how such discrepancy is defined. Indeed, Blumer (1971, 301) argued that "social problems are not the result of an intrinsic malfunctioning of a society but are the result of a process of definition in which a given condition is picked out and identified as a social problem." How society identifies, defines, and legitimizes a condition determines whether it rises to a certain status to be regarded as a social problem.

An example of a social problem is global warming (McCright and Dunlap 2000). Global warming figured prominently into public consciousness, for it represented a discrepancy between an ideal situation and the current material conditions that threaten sustainability. Global warming captured the attention of natural scientists but also social scientists who sought to understand ways to get the public to recognize the problem and respond to it (McCright and Dunlap 2000). Such scholarly and public attention conferred on global warming the status of a legitimate social concern, but it also sparked a countermovement to question its legitimacy (McCright and Dunlap 2000). Indeed, the process of legitimation is integral for a problem to merit public attention and action. "If the social problem fails to get legitimacy, it flounders and languishes outside of the arena of public action" (Blumer 1971, 303). Indeed, Hilgartner and Bosk (1988, 55) defined a social problem "as a putative condition or situation that is labeled a problem in the arenas of public discourse and action." Furthermore, they argued that "public attention is a scarce resource" and therefore social problems are also determined through symbolic competition in public arenas (55). These public arenas, where the "collective definition of social problems occurs," refer to different public spaces where people engage in symbolic contests (58). A common public arena is the news media (Hilgartner and Bosk 1988). For example, Schneider (1985, 221) argued that in many instances, those involved in, or confronted by, social problems "hope the news media will help them publicize claims and thus enhance their legitimacy." This function of the news media can be seen in the multitude of studies that focused on analyzing the news coverage of particular social problems, such as wars (Iyengar and Simon 1993), crimes (Marsh 1991), environmental issues (Trumbo 1996), and health problems (Kim and Willis 2007). These and other similar studies highlight the important role of journalists in co-defining and legitimizing social problems, which contributes to focusing public attention and response on them.

### *Problems Journalists Face*

Journalists themselves are social actors working within organizational and social contexts that also expose them to a host of different problems. While they help to define and legitimize social problems, journalists also face problems in their profession. Studies have documented the different problems that journalists face, such as those arising from changes in technology (Garrison 2000; Singer 1997), from gender differences, particularly in covering sports (Miller and Miller 1995; Salwen and Garrison 1998), and from covering disasters and other traumatic events (Cottle 2013; Dworznik 2006). For example, a survey of sports journalists found that for journalism in general, reader-related issues, problems with professionalism, and increased competition were considered the most important (Salwen and Garrison 1998). A study about journalists and their relationship with public relations practitioners identified five major problems associated with newspaper work: "long hours; lack of job security; unpleasant assignments; incessant work demands; and negative reputations" (DeLorme and Fedler 2003, 108). Covering disasters also forces journalists to wrestle between objectivity as a norm and being part of the affected community (Littlefield and Quenette 2007). This is on top of the physical and psychological trauma they experience (Weidmann, Fehm, and Fydrich 2008).

Understanding journalists' work problems is important because these problems affect various aspects of journalists' work, such as their attitude toward public relations (DeLorme and Fedler 2003; Yun and Yoon 2011). Going by the assumption of the sociology of social problems, a crucial step in addressing a social problem is its definition (Hilgartner and Bosk 1988). Thus, for the problems confronting journalists to be legitimized, they should first be clearly defined by journalists themselves, who are used to co-defining and legitimizing social problems that they cover as news. This process of self-definition is consistent with the idea that journalists are part of an interpretive community (Zelizer 1993, 2010). An interpretive community is defined as "a cultural site where meanings are constructed, shared, and reconstructed by members of social groups in the course of everyday life" (Berkowitz and TerKeurst 1999, 125). Indeed, journalists not only help construct social problems of the people and institutions they cover, they also engage in deliberations about the problems they themselves face as a community (Zelizer 1992).

This conceptualization is also consistent with the idea of journalism as a field, which agents seek to either transform or preserve (Bourdieu 1998, 2005). Being a field of constant struggle, journalism is also a field of problems that agents have to navigate. For instance, the journalistic field is caught between two forms of capital: economic and cultural (Benson and Neveu 2005a). While economic capital refers to revenues and audience shares that sustain the field financially, cultural capital refers to the knowledge and skills unique to the field that confer it with legitimacy and credibility (Benson 2006). Therefore, pursuit of economic capital often exposes the field to external forces, such as advertisers, while the pursuit of cultural capital is often associated with preserving the field's autonomy (Benson and Neveu 2005b). While one form of capital can be converted into the other, they might also be incompatible at times. For example, the Philippine media system is dominated by news outlets owned by wealthy families with other non-media business interests, an ownership pattern that exposes journalists to the strong sway of economic capital, threatening their autonomy, as owners not only seek profit from their media business but also use their news outlets in protecting their other business interests (Coronel 2001). Guided by the definition of social problems of journalists who are members of an interpretive community, existing in a field of constant struggle, this study seeks to uncover what problems journalists in the Philippines consider to be most important within their journalistic community.

### *The Philippine Press*

The history of Philippine journalism is marked by numerous struggles against oppression. For example, *La Solidaridad*, the most popular newspaper to emerge from the Spanish colonial period, was first published in 1889 as the official paper of a reform movement that questioned the abuses of the Spanish regime (Ables 2003; Maslog 1994; Quintos De Jesus 2004). During the Japanese occupation between 1942 and 1945, an underground press flourished to support the guerilla movement against the Japanese forces (Quintos De Jesus 2004). The Marcos dictatorship, which began with the declaration of Martial Law in 1972, also saw the rise of the so-called *mosquito press* that questioned the government, resisted media censorship, and provided an alternative to mainstream media that were friendly to the regime (Gonzalez 1988; Maslog 1994).

The Philippine media system is patterned after that of the United States, which occupied the country from 1898 to 1946. The People Power revolution that toppled the Marcos dictatorship in 1986 gave rise to a media system that vigorously maximized and protected its newfound freedom. However, Philippine society continues to be ruled by an oligarchy, with its economy—and its media—controlled by a handful of wealthy families (Rosales 2006). Therefore, "the media have also used their freedoms to outdo rivals in the race to peddle newspapers and television programs," leading to sensationalism and homogeneous reporting (Coronel 2001, 118). "The result is the tabloidization of news and public affairs" (118). The Philippine press is also marked by a heavy focus on politics, crime, and sex. It is also characterized by an obsession with media personalities, with movie stars, and even broadcast journalists successfully crossing over to politics by taking advantage of their mass media status (Tandoc and Skoric 2010).

National newspapers, aimed at educated and elite readers, are published in English, a remnant of the 50-year American occupation of the archipelago. Tabloids, which outsell broadsheets, are published in the vernacular, targeting low-income readers with crime stories and sexually suggestive photos on their front pages. Television, which broadcasts in the vernacular, remains the most popular medium for national news. Local radio also remains popular, but only for niche news audiences, usually defined by geographic region, so many of these local stations broadcast in regional dialects (Rosales 2006; Sussman 1991).

Still a developing economy, the Philippines lacks an economic base to provide decent salaries to most journalists, particularly those working outside Metro Manila, the country's financial and political capital (Shafer 1990). This has made provincial journalists prone to corruption. For example, a common practice among some journalists is "envelopmental journalism," a play on developmental journalism (Shafer 1990). This refers to accepting or even extorting bribes, usually in envelopes, to either attack or defend someone in the media. Such practice is closely linked to media violence, usually perpetrated by local warlords and public officials. Local journalists who refuse bribes put their lives at risk, targeted by politicians and warlords unhappy with critical reporting (Rosales 2006). Those who accept bribes, however, are also at the mercy of those who pay them. The politicians and warlords who bribe journalists expect only positive coverage from them, and any departure is usually met with threats and attacks. Local journalists also lack the organizational protection and support that national journalists enjoy, making them more vulnerable to violence.

Many of the journalists killed in the country were local radio journalists. This is partly because "radio is the king of all media in the Philippines, especially in the provinces" (Rosales 2006, 148). Some of these slain radio announcers were aggressive critics of local politicians. Some of them also engaged in investigative journalism to expose corruption and illegal activities. What aggravates the situation is the weak judicial system, with many cases of violence against journalists still unresolved (Rosales 2006). An example is the Maguindanao Massacre, where 32 of the 57 people killed were journalists. Seven years after the massacre, no one has been convicted, with the trial marked by delays, killing of key witnesses, and the death of the alleged mastermind in 2015 of heart attack (Whaley 2015). The rising number of cases of violence against journalists is reflected in many international rankings that consider the Philippine press as only "partly free" (e.g. Freedom House 2015), and yet some argued that the spate of media killings in the country does not constitute state repression (Aguilar, Mendoza, and Candelaria 2014). Many of these cases were local in context: "The killing could be a form of repression but not one directed by the central state" (651). However, the same study argued that "broad structural factors" have allowed "an atmosphere of impunity that perpetuates these killings" (673).

One of these structural factors could very well be the lack of a freedom of information (FOI) law in the Philippines. Since democracy rests on the power of the people, some of which is conferred on their chosen representatives in the government, then they are also entitled to freely obtain information collected and held by the same government that they have authorized. This access to information enables citizens to better evaluate and hold accountable the government that supposedly works for them (Michener 2011; Vleugels 2011). An FOI law legally empowers the public to "ask for and receive information held by public bodies" (Holsen 2007, 50). Journalists, reporting on behalf of the public, also benefit from an FOI law. However, despite aggressive lobbying from journalists in the Philippines and pending legislation in Congress, the Philippine government has not passed an FOI law. Thus, journalists resort to other means of obtaining information from the government, such as getting close to sources, which also makes them more vulnerable to corruption.

### *Theoretical Synthesis*

Journalists play an integral role in defining and legitimizing social problems, and yet they are also confronted by problems of their own profession. Understanding such problems is important, because they can affect how journalists do their work. An important step in addressing a problem is socially defining it first. This exploratory study is focused on what journalists in the Philippines define as the important problems they face in their work. This is a first step in recognizing—and legitimizing—the issues encountered by journalists in the Philippines, a country with a press system marked by contradictions. This is also consistent with conceptualizing journalists as members of an interpretive community engaged in making sense of the issues that surround their profession. Therefore, this study seeks to answer the following research questions:

**RQ1:** What do journalists in the Philippines define as the most important problem they face as journalists?

**RQ2:** What individual and organizational factors affect such perceptions?

## Method

This exploratory study is based on an online survey of journalists in the Philippines. In the absence of a media directory that lists all news organizations and journalists in the country, the study adopted a multi-stage sampling strategy. First, two graduate students compiled a list of all news organizations in the country per region based on information from various sources, such as online databases, incomplete lists from organizations of journalists, and personal communication with provincial correspondents. This process mapped out 701 news organizations from all over the country. Second, based on the distribution of news organizations reflecting medium and region, a random sample of organizations was drawn. Third, requests were sent to the randomly selected news organizations for a list and contact details of all their journalists, including reporters and editors, but excluding photojournalists. Finally, randomly selected journalists from each selected news organization were invited to participate in the online survey between May and December 2015. From the 672 emails successfully sent, 349 respondents completed the online survey, for a completion rate of 52 percent.

In terms of medium, 45.3 percent worked for daily newspapers, 18.9 percent for television, 16 percent for newspaper or television websites, while 12.6 percent worked for online-only outlets. In terms of position, 56.1 percent were reporters, while 22.5 percent were editors, ranging from chief editor to senior editor. In terms of reach, 59.3 percent worked for national organizations, 21.8 percent worked for outlets with a transnational reach, while 18.3 percent worked for local or regional outlets. The sample is 51.1 percent female and the average age was 38 years old.

### *Defining Problems*

The survey used in this study is part of the Worlds of Journalism study, a larger project involving researchers from more than 70 countries. The researchers used the same questionnaire, but were allowed to include questions unique to their respective countries. This current study is based on responses to an open-ended question: "What would you say is the most important problem that journalists in the Philippines are facing?" This question was only asked in the Philippines. Since English is an official language in the Philippines, the questionnaire was distributed in English.

The respondents were asked to type in their answers using their own words. There was no specified format. This allowed the respondents to freely respond to the question, unrestricted by any prior categorization. The open-ended responses were then coded by the researcher using the constant comparative strategy often employed in qualitative studies using the grounded theory approach (Glaser 1965; Glaser and Strauss 1967). The researcher coded each response in relation to the preceding response to check whether the current response fits a previous code, requires a modification of a previous code, or merits a new code (Tracy 2013). Such process was repeated constantly until all responses were coded. A combination of *in vivo* coding (or using the respondents' own words or labels) and theoretical coding (or coding based on sensitizing concepts from the literature) was employed (Saldaña 2009; Tracy 2013). This qualitative analysis identified the following problems.

*Low pay.* This category refers to inadequate salaries as well as poor working conditions. Many journalists simply wrote "compensation" in response to the question. One respondent wrote: "I think it's the poor compensation for journalists and media workers in general."

*Corruption.* This refers to the problem of journalists accepting bribes, which many respondents considered to be unethical. Some journalists simply wrote "corruption" in their responses. One respondent wrote: "Most of the journalists today engage in 'envelopmental' journalism, trading their stories for some sort of personal gratification rather than serving the public."

*Violence.* This category refers to threats and attacks against journalists. Some respondents simply wrote "media killings" or "journalist killings." One respondent also wrote: "Impunity, the continued, unresolved killings of journalists, especially those in the provinces."

*Sensationalism.* This category refers to problems associated with journalistic practice and output, particularly in the erosion of quality. For example, a respondent wrote: "editors selling out and going for click-worthy garbage instead of socially relevant stories." Another respondent said: "The tendency to sensationalize stories to increase ratings and viewership."

*Information access.* This category refers to difficulties in getting information from the government. Many responses under this category were about the lack of an FOI law in the Philippines. For example, one respondent wrote: "Access to public information. It's very hard to pursue a relevant story because the source/document is not available." Others cited pressure from government sources who withhold relevant information.

*Business pressure.* This category refers to the perceived influence of business owners and their pursuit of financial considerations. One respondent wrote: "Rising profit motive. Meddling owners. Only three big groups controlling media … " While sensationalism as a problem referred to the quality of actual outputs, this category refers to the specific influence of owners interfering in the editorial process.

*Audience and new technology.* Others identified the pressure coming from the increasing influence of audiences enabled by new technologies. For example, one respondent wrote: "Adapting to technology because of the digital age." Another respondent wrote: "Catching up with technology and innovation; creating processes around it." Another respondent identified "the expectations of a constantly evolving audience" as the most important problem that journalists face.

*Professionalism.* This category refers to problems associated with the reputation and conduct of journalists in the country, with some respondents lamenting the erosion in media credibility. One respondent said: "The so-called citizen journalism has given birth to a new-breed of quasi-journalists who lack not only skills, but also knowledge of traditional media ethics." While sensationalism refers to the quality of output, this category specifically refers to threats to integrity and professionalism of journalists in terms of how they conduct themselves and how that reflects on the field as a whole. For example, another respondent said: "Lack of healthy skepticism and failure to challenge sources, information, and data."

### *Quantitative Analysis*

Following the qualitative coding, the researcher then quantitatively coded the responses, assigning them to the main categories of identified problems. A response might mention multiple problems, but it was coded based on the dominant problem mentioned. Dominance was determined based on which problem was mentioned first, and which problem merited a longer discussion. Since only one variable was to be coded, and given the small sample size, only one researcher conducted the quantitative analysis for this exploratory study. Ensuring reliability in this set-up required the researcher to "recode some of the earlier material and compare" (Stempel 2003, 216). Thus, the researcher recoded the same responses (about 10 percent of the data) four weeks after the initial coding. This is also referred to as ensuring intracoder reliability, which assesses the consistency in the evaluation of a particular coder over time (Neuendorf 2016). The coding process for this variable was found to be reliable, Krippendorf's alpha = 0.92.

Next, logistic regression was used to analyze the effects of individual and organizational factors—age, gender, salary, rank, employment type, and organization's reach—on the perception of the four most important problems identified. Salary was measured using a 10-point scale, from 1 (below $160 per month) to 10 (more than $1437 per month). Rank was measured by first asking for the journalist's specific position, and then recoding the responses into rank-and-file (e.g. reporter), junior manager (e.g. department head), or senior manager (e.g. chief editor). Employment type was either part-time or full-time while organization's reach was measured as local, regional, national, or transnational. Local referred to a reach confined within a particular city or municipality. Regional referred to a reach confined within a cluster of cities, municipalities, or provinces. National referred to reaching the whole country. Finally, transnational reach referred to regularly reaching populations outside the Philippines. The categorization was mainly based on the original platform. For example, a television station is classified as national when its news programs primarily target and reach viewers all over the country. While some of its news reports are uploaded on YouTube, through which it can potentially reach viewers outside the country, YouTube is not its primary platform.

## Results

RQ1 asked about the problem journalists in the Philippines defined as the most important. Following the qualitative coding of the open-ended responses, a quantitative content analysis was conducted to assign each response to one of the eight categories of problems mapped out. The most important problem was low pay, identified by 38.2 percent of the respondents. Media violence was next, identified by 20.9 percent of the respondents. This was followed by information access, identified by 9.5 percent of the respondents, and professionalism, identified by 8.5 percent of the respondents. The complete list is shown in Table 1.

RQ2 asked about the impact of individual and organizational factors on the perception of these problems. The analysis focuses on only the four most important problems

**TABLE 1**
Problems confronting journalists

| Problem | Percentage |
|---|---|
| Low pay | 38.2 |
| Media violence | 20.9 |
| Information access | 9.5 |
| Professionalism | 8.5 |
| Audience and new technology | 7.5 |
| Corruption | 6.5 |
| Business pressure | 5.2 |
| Sensationalism | 3.6 |

identified by the respondents: low pay, media violence, information access, and professionalism. The study used logistic regression to predict identification of each of these problems based on individual and organizational factors, particularly age, gender, salary, rank, type of employment, and reach of the organization. A stepwise method, using likelihood ratio statistic, was used, given the exploratory nature of the analyses (Field 2009).

The first model sought to account for influences on identifying low pay as a problem. The data fits the model well, $\chi^2(2) = 9.82$, $p < 0.01$, accounting for between 3 percent (Cox & Snell $R^2$) and 5 percent (Nagelkerke $R^2$) of the variance. However, only age ($B = -0.03$) and salary ($B = -0.05$) were significant predictors (see Table 2). That is, younger journalists with lower salaries tend to identify low wages as the most important problem. The model was able to make correct outcome predictions at 63 percent.

The second model sought to account for influences on identifying media violence as a problem. The data also fits the model well, $\chi^2(1) = 5.52$, $p < 0.05$, but only accounting for between 2 percent (Cox & Snell $R^2$) and 3 percent (Nagelkerke $R^2$) of the variance. Only rank ($B = -0.64$) was a significant predictor (see Table 2). That is, reporters more than senior editors and managers tend to identify media violence as the most important problem. The model was able to make correct outcome predictions at 80 percent.

The third model sought to account for influences on identifying information access as a problem. The logistic regression model, however, does not fit the data well.

**TABLE 2**
Predicting identification of problems

| | Low pay | Violence | Professionalism |
|---|---|---|---|
| Age | −0.03 | | |
| Gender | | | |
| Salary | −0.11 | | 0.14 |
| Employment status | | | |
| Rank | | −0.64 | |
| Organization's reach | | | |
| Cox & Snell $R^2$ | 0.03 | 0.02 | 0.01 |
| Nagelkerke $R^2$ | 0.05 | 0.03 | 0.03 |

The coefficients reported here are unstandardized beta values based on logistic regression. The coefficients are all significant, $p < 0.05$. Non-significant effects are excluded, consistent with the results of using the stepwise method.

Finally, the fourth model sought to account for influences on identifying threats to professionalism as a problem. The data also fits the model well, $\chi^2(1) = 3.94$, $p < 0.05$, accounting for between 1 percent (Cox & Snell $R^2$) and 3 percent (Nagelkerke $R^2$) of the variance. Only salary ($B = 0.14$) was a significant predictor (see Table 2). That is, the higher a journalist's salary, the more likely he or she is to identify professionalism as the most important problem facing journalists. The model was able to make correct outcome predictions at 91.4 percent.

## Discussion and Conclusion

This study explored what Filipino journalists considered to be the most important problem they are facing as a community, and what individual and organizational factors affect such perceptions. The analysis found that the four most important problems identified by the respondents were low pay, violence against journalists, difficulties in information access, and professionalism. Younger journalists tend to identify low pay as the most important problem, while those with higher salaries tend to identify threats to professionalism as the most important. The problem of violence against journalists was more salient for reporters than for editors and managers.

Defining a problem is a crucial step in conceptualizing it as a social problem that merits public attention and response (Kitsuse and Spector 1973). By analyzing what journalists identify as the most important problem they face, this study sought to document this process of definition and to contribute to the process of legitimation. The approach taken here—using an open-ended question that allowed the respondents to articulate their answers using their own words and without the constraint of pre-selected categories—allowed the respondents to freely identify and define the social problems that confront the journalistic community in the Philippines. The problems they identified demonstrate discrepancies from what they consider to be the ideal and their actual conditions. This identification is consistent with defining social problems (Fuller and Myers 1941). While journalists form a small part of the population, the problems they face are important to define and address, considering the important role they play and the power they possess in young democracies such as the Philippines.

The results are consistent with the ongoing discourse among Filipino journalists documented by previous academic studies and even news articles. First, some 38 percent identified low pay as the most important problem. This is consistent with what studies have documented in the past (Rosales 2006; Shafer 1990). This is rather unfortunate, for it demonstrates how the problem of inadequate salaries has persisted and has remained unchecked. This problem is largely structural, with the Philippine economy remaining unable to sufficiently support workers across different industries, including the media (Shafer and Aregood 2012). This is also worrisome, considering the link between low wages and media corruption (Shafer 1990). Inadequate pay makes journalists more vulnerable to accepting bribes. The analysis found that younger journalists were more likely than older journalists to identify low wages as the most important problem. First, this perception points to low starting salaries for journalists in the Philippines. While salaries increase the longer one stays in journalism, low starting pay can potentially serve as a barrier to attracting young journalists. Second, older journalists, who have stayed in the profession for quite some time, are likely to have had experienced and survived relatively meager incomes.

Thus, the problem of low pay is not as salient for them anymore as it is currently for their younger colleagues.

Second, some 21 percent identified violence against journalists as the most important problem. This shows that journalists themselves recognize the importance and the seriousness of the unabated killing of journalists in the Philippines that international agencies have recognized and documented (Freedom House 2015; IFJ 2016). While most of the journalists killed in the country were those working in the provinces outside the nation's political capital, organization's reach, which also measured the geographic base of the journalists who responded to the survey, was not a significant predictor of identifying media killing as the most important problem. This is actually an encouraging finding, as it shows that many journalists, regardless of whether they belong to local or national outlets, recognize the problem of violence against the press. Rank was a significant predictor: reporters were more likely to identify media violence as the most important problem than were editors and managers. This is plausibly because reporters, who are at the frontlines of day-to-day journalism, dealing with sources and interacting with public officials routinely, feel more vulnerable to these kinds of attacks. The violence perpetrated against journalists is an important problem, as it can also have a chilling effect among current and future journalists. For example, current journalists might be more wary about exercising their watchdog role, for fear of being attacked (Rosales 2006). Those considering journalism as a career might also think twice about joining the profession, given the level of impunity with which attacks on media workers are carried out in the country.

Respondents ranked information access as the third most important problem. Many of the responses under this category referred to the lack of an FOI law in the Philippines. Without a law that guarantees people's right to information, journalists in the Philippines have to find other ways of obtaining information for their reports. While it is a good test for a journalist's resourcefulness and ability to establish good rapport with sources, this set-up also puts journalists at the mercy, and sometimes under the control, of government officials. When journalists become too dependent on particular sources for information, which could have been freely obtained using an FOI act, they also become vulnerable to misinformation as well as to the agenda of their sources. Older democracies have instituted FOI laws with good results (McClean 2010; Michener 2011), and the Philippine government should examine these examples. The country's guarantee of press freedom, provided in the Constitution, can only be maximized if government information is made available to the public, often represented by journalists. This is also consistent with transparent governance.

Fourth, some 9 percent of the respondents identified threats to professionalism as the most important problem, and salary was a positive predictor. That is, journalists with higher salaries tend to identify professionalism as the most serious issue more than those with lower salaries. This is an interesting finding, which future studies should explore. It seems that journalists with higher economic capital, based on their salaries, are able to focus and reflect on journalism's credibility, a measure of cultural capital. It appears that journalists who feel secure of their economic capital are able to consider issues about the field's cultural capital more than journalists confronted with an unstable economic capital (Benson and Neveu 2005b).

The problems identified by the respondents in the survey can also be classified based on two theoretical considerations (see Table 3). First, the problems can be classified as issues concerning the field's economic or cultural capital. For example, the problem of low wages focuses on the issue of a low economic capital for journalism which is felt down to the individual level. On the other hand, the problem with professionalism can be classified under cultural capital. Second, the problems identified by journalists can also be classified as either internal to the field or brought by external forces. For example, sensationalism is a problem perpetrated by journalists, while media violence is perpetrated by external forces, such as public officials. Such conceptual mapping of the problems identified by journalists demonstrates how most of the problems identified are external, perpetrated by outside forces (see Table 3). This is an initial step in identifying where and how response could and should begin. For example, the government can extend support by looking into the problems of media killings and information access. Organizations should also look into the issues of low pay, but the government should also institutionalize measures to protect the welfare of those working as journalists.

It is also noteworthy that the three most important problems identified by the respondents were perpetrated by external forces or linked to a lack of sufficient structural support from institutions external to the journalistic field, such as the government. This offers a closer look into how journalists engage in introspection. It appears that in reflecting about the problems concerning the field of journalism, journalists focus more on how external forces negatively affect their work than on the problems generated internally within the journalistic field by journalists themselves. But while journalists are socialized into protecting their fragile autonomy, they also need support from various social institutions. While they need to protect their work from external influence, journalists also appear to recognize that to carry out their work they also need support from other social institutions.

The findings of this study should be examined in the context of several limitations. First, the use of the survey method allowed the study to reach many journalists across platforms, positions, and geographic locations, but this was at the expense of depth. While the respondents were allowed to freely answer the open-ended question using their own words, they might have been limited by time, given that the question was one of several asked in the online survey. Thus, future studies should consider conducting respondent interviews to allow for follow-up questions as well as to delve in deeper into the responses. Second, given the exploratory nature of the study, only a few individual and organizational variables were included in the analysis to predict identification of the problems. This limitation can be seen in the rather small percentages of variance explained. Future studies can build on the conceptualization of journalists' problems proposed in this study and explore

**TABLE 3**
Conceptual mapping of problems

| | Internal agents | External forces |
|---|---|---|
| Economic | Corruption | Business pressure<br>Low pay |
| Cultural | Sensationalism<br>Professionalism | Audience and new technology<br>Media violence<br>Information access |

The problems identified by the respondents can be classified based on two theoretical considerations. First, the problems can be classified as issues concerning the field's economic or cultural capital. Second, the problems can be classified as either internal to the field or brought by external forces. For example, sensationalism is a problem perpetrated by journalists, while media violence is perpetrated by external forces.

the impact of other variables, including country-level variables, given that many of the problems identified are plausibly explained by lack of structural, national-level support. Third, this exploratory study focused only on what problems journalists in the Philippines considered to be most important. While this is a crucial step in elevating such problems into social problems to merit attention and response, an important assumption not tested in this study is how such problems affect the extent to which journalists can effectively do their work. Thus, future studies can build on the conceptualization of problems proposed here in exploring how particular problems affect journalistic practice. Finally, this study focused only on journalists from the Philippines. It is plausible that the problems defined by journalists in the Philippines also confront journalists in other media systems. But it is also plausible that particular problems are endemic only in media systems similar to that in the Philippines. Future studies can build on the findings of this exploratory study to examine problems confronting journalists in other countries and other media systems. Despite these limitations, this study hopes to be able to contribute to understanding the problems that journalists face, particularly in a media context such as that in the Philippines. This understanding can hopefully contribute not only to increased awareness of the plight of journalists in the Philippines, but also to an increased concern and collective response among the public and the government to also watch over the watchdogs.

## DISCLOSURE STATEMENT

No potential conflict of interest was reported by the author.

## REFERENCES

Ables, Higinon. 2003. *Mass Communication and Philippine Society*. Quezon City: University of the Philippines Press.

Aguilar, Filomeno V., Meynardo P. Mendoza, and Anne Lan K. Candelaria. 2014. "Keeping the State at Bay: The Killing of Journalists in the Philippines, 1998–2012." *Critical Asian Studies* 46 (4): 649–677. doi:10.1080/14672715.2014.960719.

Benson, Rodney. 2006. "News Media as a "Journalistic Field": What Bourdieu Adds to New Institutionalism, and Vice Versa." *Political Communication* 23 (2): 187–202. doi:10.1080/10584600600629802.

Benson, Rodney, and Erik Neveu, eds. 2005a. *Bourdieu and the Journalistic Field*. Malden, MA: Polity Press.

Benson, Rodney, and Erik Neveu. 2005b. "Introduction: Field Theory as a Work in Progress." In *Bourdieu and the Journalistic Field*, edited by Rodney Benson and Erik Neveu, 1–28. Malden, MA: Polity Press.

Berkowitz, Dan, and James V. TerKeurst. 1999. "Community as Interpretive Community: Rethinking the Journalist-source Relationship." *Journal of Communication* 49 (3): 125–136. doi:10.1111/j.1460-2466.1999.tb02808.x.

Blumer, Herbert. 1971. "Social Problems as Collective Behavior." *Social Problems* 18 (3): 298–306. doi:10.2307/799797.

Bourdieu, Pierre. 1998. *On Television*. New York: The New Press.

Bourdieu, Pierre. 2005. "The Political Field, the Social Science Field and the Journalistic Field." In *Bourdieu and the Journalistic Field*, edited by Rodney Benson and Erik Neveu, 29–47. Malden, MA: Polity Press.

Coronel, Sheila S. 2001. "The Media, the Market and Democracy: The Case of the Philippines." *Javnost – The Public* 8 (2): 109–126. doi:10.1080/13183222.2001.11008774.

Cottle, Simon. 2013. "Journalists Witnessing Disaster: From the Calculus of Death to the Injunction to Care." *Journalism Studies* 14 (2): 232–248. doi:10.1080/1461670X.2012.718556.

DeLorme, Denise E., and Fred Fedler. 2003. "Journalists' Hostility Toward Public Relations: An Historical Analysis." *Public Relations Review* 29 (2): 99–124. doi:http://dx.doi.org/10.1016/S0363-8111(03)00019-5.

Dworznik, Gretchen. 2006. "Journalism and Trauma: How Reporters and Photographers Make Sense of What They See." *Journalism Studies* 7 (4): 534–553. doi:10.1080/14616700600757977.

Field, Andy. 2009. *Discovering Statistics Using SPSS*. 3rd ed. Thousand Oaks, CA: Sage.

Freedom House. 2015. Philippines. *Freedom of the Press 2016*, https://freedomhouse.org/report/freedom-press/2015/philippines.

Fuller, Richard C., and Richard R. Myers. 1941. "The Natural History of a Social Problem." *American Sociological Review* 6 (3): 320–329. doi:10.2307/2086189.

Garrison, Bruce. 2000. "Journalists' Perceptions of Online Information-gathering Problems." *Journalism & Mass Communication Quarterly* 77 (3): 500–514. doi:10.1177/107769900007700303.

Glaser, Barney G. 1965. "The Constant Comparative Method of Qualitative Analysis." *Social Problems* 12 (4): 436–445.

Glaser, Barney G., and Anselm Strauss. 1967. *The Discovery of Grounded Theory: Strategies for Qualitative Research*. London: Weidenfeld and Nicolson.

Gonzalez, Hernando. 1988. "Mass Media and the Spiral of Silence: The Philippines from Marcos to Aquino." *Journal of Communication* 38 (4): 33–48. doi:10.1111/j.1460-2466.1988.tb02068.x.

Hilgartner, Stephen, and Charles L. Bosk. 1988. "The Rise and Fall of Social Problems: A Public Arenas Model." *American Journal of Sociology* 94 (1): 53–78.

Holsen, Sarah. 2007. "Freedom of Information in the U.K., U.S., and Canada." *Information Management Journal* 41 (3): 50–55.

IFJ (International Federation of Journalists). 2016. "At least 2297 Journalists and Media Staff have been Killed Since 1990". http://ifj-safety.org/en/contents/at-least-2297-journalists-and-media-staff-have-been-killed-since-1990-ifj-report.

Iyengar, Shanto, and Adam Simon. 1993. "News Coverage of the Gulf Crisis and Public Opinion: A Study of Agenda-setting, Priming, and Framing." *Communication Research* 20 (3): 365–383.

Kim, Sei-Hill, and L. Anne Willis. 2007. "Talking About Obesity: News Framing of who is Responsible for Causing and Fixing the Problem." *Journal of Health Communication* 12 (4): 359–376. doi:10.1080/10810730701326051.

Kitsuse, John I., and Malcolm Spector. 1973. "Toward a Sociology of Social Problems: Social Conditions, Value-judgments, and Social Problems." *Social Problems* 20 (4): 407–419. doi:10.2307/799704.

Littlefield, Robert S., and Andrea M. Quenette. 2007. "Crisis Leadership and Hurricane Katrina: The Portrayal of Authority by the Media in Natural Disasters." *Journal of Applied Communication Research* 35 (1): 26–47. doi:10.1080/00909880601065664.

Marsh, Harry L. 1991. "A Comparative Analysis of Crime Coverage in Newspapers in the United States and Other Countries from 1960–1989: A Review of the Literature." *Journal of Criminal Justice* 19 (1): 67–79. doi:http://dx.doi.org/10.1016/0047-2352(91)90083-8.

Maslog, Crispin. 1994. *The Metro Manila Press*. Manila: Philippine Press Institute.

McClean, Tom. 2010. "Who Pays the Piper? The Political Economy of Freedom of Information." *Government Information Quarterly* 27 (4): 392–400. doi:10.1016/j.giq.2010.05.004.

McCright, Aaron M., and Riley E. Dunlap. 2000. "Challenging Global Warming as a Social Problem: An Analysis of the Conservative Movement's Counter-claims." *Social Problems* 47 (4): 499–522. doi:10.2307/3097132.

Merton, Robert, and Robert Nisbet. 1976. *Contemporary Social Problems*. Vol. 2. New York: Harcourt Brace Jovanovich.

Michener, Greg. 2011. "FOI Laws Around the World." *Journal of Democracy* 22 (2): 145–159.

Miller, Phyllis, and Randy Miller. 1995. "The Invisible Woman: Female Sports Journalists in the Workplace." *Journalism & Mass Communication Quarterly* 72 (4): 883–889.

Neuendorf, Kimberly. 2016. *The Content Analysis Guidebook*. 2nd ed. Los Angeles, CA: SAGE Publications.

Quintos De Jesus, Melinda. 2004. *Press Freedom in the Philippines: A Study in Contradictions*. Manila: Center for Media Freedom and Responsibility.

Rauhala, Emily. 2014. It's been Five Years Since the Maguindanao Massacre and the Perpetrators are Still Free. *Time*, http://time.com/3598796/its-been-five-years-since-the-maguindanao-massacre-and-the-perpetrators-are-still-free/.

Rosales, Rey G. 2006. "Shooting the Messenger: Why Radio Broadcasting is a Deadly Profession in the Philippines." *Journal of Radio Studies* 13 (1): 146–155. doi:10.1207/s15506843jrs1301_10.

Saldaña, Johnny. 2009. *The Coding Manual for Qualitative Researchers*. Thousand Oaks, CA: Sage.

Salwen, Michael B., and Bruce Garrison. 1998. "Finding their Place in Journalism: Newspaper Sports Journalists' Professional "Problems'." *Journal of Sport & Social Issues* 22 (1): 88–102. doi:10.1177/019372398022001008.

Schneider, Joseph W. 1985. "Social Problems Theory: The Constructionist View." *Annual Review of Sociology* 11 (1): 209–229. doi:10.1146/annurev.so.11.080185.001233.

Shafer, Richard. 1990. "Greasing the Newsgate: Journalist on the Take in the Philippines." *Journal of Mass Media Ethics* 5 (1): 15–29. doi:10.1207/s15327728jmme0501_2.

Shafer, Richard, and Richard Aregood. 2012. "Protecting Journalists by Applying the Civic Journalism Model in Developing Countries: A Case Study of the Philippines." *Media Asia* 39 (2): 93–98. doi:10.1080/01296612.2012.11689923.

Singer, Jane B. 1997. "Changes and Consistencies: Newspaper Journalists Contemplate Online Future." *Newspaper Research Journal* 18 (1–2): 2–18.

Stempel, Guido. 2003. "Content Analysis." In *Mass Communication Research and Theory*, edited by Guido Stempel, David Weaver, and G. Cleveland Wilhoit, 209–219. Boston, MA: Pearson Education.

Sussman, Leonard R. 1991. "Dying (and Being Killed) on the Job: A Case Study of World Journalists, 1982–1989." *Journalism & Mass Communication Quarterly* 68 (1–2): 195–199. doi:10.1177/107769909106800121.

Tandoc, Edson C. 2014. "Journalism is Twerking? How web Analytics is Changing the Process of Gatekeeping." *New Media & Society* 16 (4): 559–575. doi:10.1177/1461444814530541.

Tandoc, Edson, and Marko Skoric. 2010. "The Pseudo-events Paradox: How Pseudo-events Flood the Philippine Press and why Journalists Don't Recognize it." *Asian Journal of Communication* 20 (1): 33–50. doi:10.1080/01292980903440830.

Tracy, Sarah. 2013. *Qualitative Research Methods: Collecting Evidence, Crafting Analysis, Communicating Impact*. Malden, MA: Wiley-Blackwell.

Trumbo, Craig. 1996. "Constructing Climate Change: Claims and Frames in US News Coverage of an Environmental Issue." *Public Understanding of Science* 5 (3): 269–283. doi:10.1088/0963-6625/5/3/006.

Vleugels, Roger. 2011. "Overview of all FOI Laws." *Fringe Special*.

Weidmann, Anke, Lydia Fehm, and Thomas Fydrich. 2008. "Covering the Tsunami Disaster: Subsequent Post-Traumatic and Depressive Symptoms and Associated Social Factors." *Stress and Health* 24 (2): 129–135. doi:10.1002/smi.1168.

Whaley, Floyd. 2015. Andal Ampatuan Sr., Suspect in Philippine Massacre, Dies during Trial. *The New York Times*, http://www.nytimes.com/2015/07/19/world/asia/andal-ampatuan-sr-suspect-in-philippine-massacre-dies-during-trial.html?_r=0.

Yun, Seong-Hun, and Heesang Yoon. 2011. "Are "Journalists' Own Problems' Aggravating their Hostility Toward Public Relations?—A Study of Korean Journalists." *Public Relations Review* 37 (3): 305–313. doi:http://dx.doi.org/10.1016/j.pubrev.2011.03.004.

Zelizer, Barbie. 1992. "CNN, the Gulf War, and Journalistic Practice." *Journal of Communication* 42 (1): 66–81. doi:10.1111/j.1460-2466.1992.tb00769.x.

Zelizer, Barbie. 1993. "Journalists as Interpretive Communities." *Critical Studies in Mass Communication* 10 (3): 219–237. doi:10.1080/15295039309366865.

Zelizer, Barbie. 2010. "Journalists as Interpretive Communities Revisited." In *The Routledge Companion to News and Journalism*, edited by Stuart Allan, 181–190. New York: Routledge.

# Index

Note: **Bold** page numbers refer to tables; *italic* page numbers refer to figures and page numbers followed by "n" denote endnotes.